Rosalie Fiorino Harpole

ROSALIE
SERVING
Country

Rosalie Fiorino Harpole

ROSALIE
SERVING
Country

Photographs by:
St. Louis Color

Graphic Design by:
Dennis Fiorini
Grafx Gourmet
grafxgourmet@yahoo.com

Proofread by:
Joni Owens

Published by:
Rosalie Fiorino Harpole
58 Madden, Troy, MO 63379

Printed by:
R. R. Donnelley & Sons
600 W State Road 32
Crawfordsville, IN 47933-8967
(765) 362-0703

Manufactured in the United States of America

ISBN-13: 978-0-615-30610-0

Library of Congress Cataloging in Publication Data

CONTENTS

DEDICATION

- This, my second cookbook, again is written for the glory of God. When I give Him my best, He gives me His supreme! With Him, all things are possible.

- To my beloved husband, Bill, who edits, compiles, indexes and taste tests all the work of my hands. He packs my books, as well as my clothes.

- To my three children and their loving spouses; Scott and Jennifer, Jeff and Tami, and Dana and David. Thanks for the joy of letting me be a part of your lives.

- To the real joys of my life, who are ten of the smartest, cutest, and sweetest grandchildren ever: Taylor Ryan Harpole, Ross David Harpole, Grant Nehemiah Carleton Harpole, Max Geoffrey Harpole, Roman Anthony Harpole, Reagan Brack Harpole, Alexandra Von Harpole, Nicholas Fiorino Harpole, Elijah Harpole Schultz, and our newest joy, Sebastian Durniat Schultz.

Top left: Reagan, Alexandra, Nicholas & Roman

Top right: Elijah & Sebastian Schultz

Bottom right: Ross, Grant, Max & Taylor

ACKNOWLEDGEMENTS

Albert Schweitzer said, "Success is not the key to happiness. Happiness is the key to success. If you love what you are doing, you will be successful." I am so blessed and fortunate to love what I do—writing cookbooks, teaching cooking classes, catering events, hosting fund raisers, speaking on family values, and serving the best food that I can possibly create.

But none of this would be possible if it were not for all the great people that have crossed my path, believed in me, and gave me opportunity to serve them with these talents. I speak of experience, having written the first cookbook, *Rosalie Serving Italian*, and now this second book, *Rosalie Serving Country*. It was the countless book signings, speaking events, TV cooking shows, radio interviews, newspaper articles, catering opportunities, and cooking classes that you, my faithful friends, have allowed me to participate in. So my acknowledgments are numerous, and forever appreciated.

To God be the glory! It is ultimately my Lord and Savior, Jesus Christ, who I must first of all thank for the health, strength, and inspiration to undertake such a feat as writing a cookbook.

Second, I again give much credit to my beloved husband, Bill, who has endured yet another two years of an office brimming with books, binders, articles, and references related to this project. I thank him for typing, editing, and indexing *Rosalie Serving Country*.

I wish to thank my immediate family, Scott and Jenn, Jeff and Tami, and David and Dana, and their children, respectively, for letting me show you off a second time by the way of pictures in my book. Without family, there would be no book.

I thank all of the staff who has allowed me to teach cooking classes: Dierbergs School of Cooking, located in the St. Louis, Missouri, and Illinois locations; Rendezvous Café, O'Fallon, Missouri; Kitchen Conservatory, St. Louis, Missouri; Whitestone Country Inn, Kingston, Tennessee; and all of the countless church and private home classes that I was able to conduct. These classes were so much fun for me and I learned as much as I taught from some of the greatest cooks in the world.

Thanks to my graphic arts designer, Dennis Fiorini, who did a beautiful job on the layout of this book. His talents are shown from the cover design to the back and all through the pages.

Thanks to my food photographer, Guillermo Gomez, owner of St. Louis Color Photography, and his faithful assistants, Sonya Dea and Stacy Collier, for all the photo shoots, beginning with the front cover, some family photos, food items, and back cover. And the many, many food shots, some done many times over. What would a cookbook be without pictures? Thanks, Guillermo, for all you do.

Thanks to my son-in-law, David Schultz, for the beautiful family shots. I loved every one of them.

Thanks to all of the doctors, nurses, technicians, therapists, and housekeepers at Lincoln County Medical Center, where I work as a registered nurse. For all the taste testing and your valuable opinions on every dish I would bring, I say thank you. They mostly gave me 10s on every recipe.

(**Acknowledgements** . . . continued on page 8)

*(**Acknowledgements** . . . continued from page 7)*

Thanks to my printer R. R. Donnelley & Sons, Crawfordsville, Indiana. You did a fantastic job on the quality of paper, laminated design, and printing of the material. Thanks, also, to Joni Owens for her help with proofreading the material.

To all those who gave endorsement of this cookbook, I so appreciated your comments.

And as with the first cookbook, *Rosalie Serving Italian,* I must give thanks for all the celebrated southern and country cooks who have gone before me on *Rosalie Serving Country*. These authors have written great and valuable books of country recipes, the country way of life and of comfort foods from generations ago. Some of my favorites are: the *Southern Living Cookbook; Secrets from the Southern Living Test Kitchens; Paula Deen* cookbooks; the *Lee Brothers Cookbook;* and my old standbys, Mark Bittman's *How to Cook Everything,* and *The Joy of Cooking.* I'm sure there are many more, but these are some of my favorites.

Endorsements

Needing a cook to oversee our Country Kitchen, the Old Thresher's Association Fair Board decided to ask Rosalie if she was up to the task. She thought about it and agreed. Much to our delight, she was terrific! Just a few of our favorites were her **Chicken and Dumplings, Home-made Bean Soup, Farmer's Cabbage, Blackberry Cobbler** and her famous **Sugar Yeast Rolls.** These alone were enough to bring the crowds back time and time again, and people would stand in line just to get a **Sugar Yeast Roll.** We can't wait to get your book, *Rosalie Serving Country;* no telling how long the line will be!

Dale Kasa
President of The Old Thresher's Association
Country Fair of Elsberry, Missouri

Whitestone Country Inn was privileged to enjoy a week of Rosalie's delicacies. Her enthusiasm as she shared her recipes and cooking techniques was contagious. She conducted classes for novices as well as our trained chefs and fellow innkeepers. After treating our staff to one of her **Raspberry Cream Cheese Custard Pies,** we decided we had to offer it to our guests. It has quickly become a favorite.

Jean Cowell, Founder and Owner
Whitestone Country Inn
Kingston, Tennessee

Rendezvous Café & Wine Bar has had the privilege of offering hands-on cooking classes with Rosalie Harpole for over a year now. Her "down to earth" approach enables our clients to identify with her. She becomes a friend from the first moment they meet her.

We have held many classes from her first cookbook, *Rosalie Serving Italian.* Every recipe she has prepared has been terrific! I have tasted some items from her new cookbook, *Rosalie Serving Country,* and am anxious for the book to be published, so everyone can experience the great culinary treats such as **Farmer's Cabbage, Chicken and Dumplings,** and the fantastic **Cinnamon Sugar Coffee Cake.**

Stephanie Thomson
Founder and Owner of Rendezvous Café, O'Fallon, Missouri

Rosalie and her wonderful recipes and cooking are legendary at our hospital and in our community. I bought her first cookbook, *Rosalie Serving Italian,* for my wife for Mother's Day, as well as for my three daughters. Soon I was having requests from all of our friends who saw the book or tried the recipes. Rosalie is also famous for her country cooking at the Old Threshers Fair, and I am predicting this new book may be even more popular than her first. I am honored to endorse your second wonderful cookbook.

Dale L. Reinker, D.O., FACO FP
Medical Director, Lincoln County Medical Center

(*Endorsements* . . . continued on page 10)

9

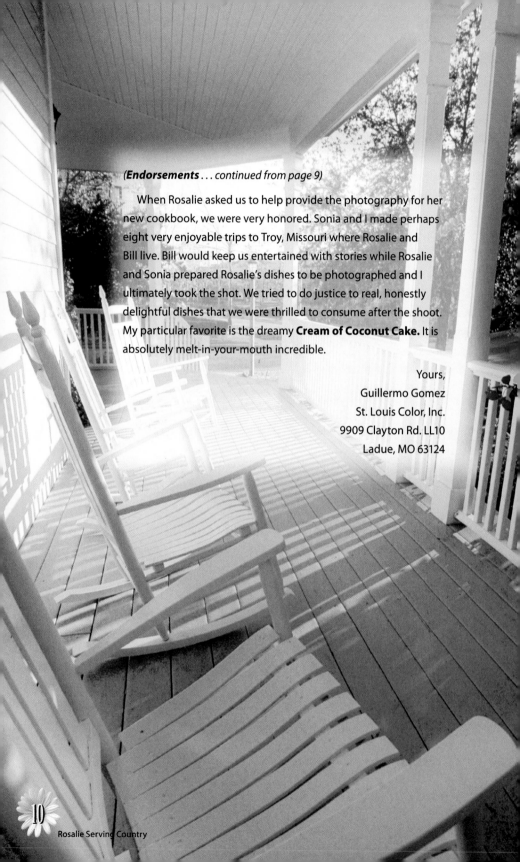

*(**Endorsements** . . . continued from page 9)*

When Rosalie asked us to help provide the photography for her new cookbook, we were very honored. Sonia and I made perhaps eight very enjoyable trips to Troy, Missouri where Rosalie and Bill live. Bill would keep us entertained with stories while Rosalie and Sonia prepared Rosalie's dishes to be photographed and I ultimately took the shot. We tried to do justice to real, honestly delightful dishes that we were thrilled to consume after the shoot. My particular favorite is the dreamy **Cream of Coconut Cake.** It is absolutely melt-in-your-mouth incredible.

Yours,
Guillermo Gomez
St. Louis Color, Inc.
9909 Clayton Rd. LL10
Ladue, MO 63124

INTRODUCTION

Writing a "Country" Cookbook has been a lot of fun for me. But there were times when I must say I've had delusions of serving **Apple Dumplings** baked in **Marinara Sauce** and **Eggplant Parmigiana** served with **Cornbread.** Even the thought of it calls for Pepto Bismal. You may ask how one who is 100 percent Italian, born and bred in the Italian culture, and steeped in olive oil, has credence to cook country cuisine.

I blame it on my husband, Bill. When he was thirty-two years old, he informed me he would oblige God and answer the call to take the pastorate of a small congregation in Troy, Missouri. The church was in need of a pastor…and wife, kids, and dog to be their spiritual leaders. (Well, maybe not the dog.) After much prayer, thought, and council, and a heartfelt invitation from the people, it was inevitable. We would be leaving the quaint suburb of St. Louis, Missouri, to go the small country town!

We had been there one year when a knock came at my door. Enter three board members of the Lincoln County Old Thresher's Association. They represented a group of farmers that display steam driven tractors, and old threshing machines, showing how to thresh wheat as they did in days gone by. This is an annual Country Fair; including the old tractors, rides for the kids, contests from quilt making to the best baked pie, and good country food. "We heard you like to cook," they said, "and we wondered if you would be the kitchen supervisor over the food this year? We need a cook, and the church could make some money." "What kind of food?", I asked. "Oh, you know, a big pot of ham and beans, fried potatoes and onions, and maybe a cobbler or two."

After much discussion, the church women and I decided we could do this! Little did I realize we would be serving 2,500 dinners in three days, or that the line formed at the kitchen door would stretch down to the old log house with seventy-five people at a time. We had 6-hour shifts of men, women, kids, and strangers, who made homemade rolls right on the spot, peeled potatoes for "real" mashed potatoes, cooked, baked, served in the dinning room, and washed pots and pans "till the cows came home."

Every year we grew more and more in popularity, listening to the fair buzz of "have you had the delicious sweet yeast rolls from the Country Kitchen?" Also, the never-ending line of people hoping to get a bowl of my creation, **Farmer's Cabbage with Short Ribs.** To say that it was a lot of work was an understatement, but the church people bonded like glue.

The last year we were in charge a dear woman came up to me and said, "Oh, I do wish we didn't have to wait another year for your good food. Why don't you just write a cookbook? That way," she said, "we will always have you with us." Driving home that day, I kept hearing her words, and as soon as I burst into the house, I said to Bill, "Guess what?" He has been packing my books almost ever since.

For information concerning my cookbooks go to my website: **www.rosalieserving.com** or contact me by email: **rosalie@rosalieserving.com**

Rosalie Serving Country

"Let's Cook Country"

From *Rosalie's Cupboard* to *Yours*

Do you ever get a longing for a country dish your mother or grandmother cooked? Maybe it's those savory **Ham & Beans** or **Creamy Macaroni & Cheese,** or even the simplest of things like a big glass of **Sweet Tea.** With a few ingredients added to your pantry or cupboard over a period of time, you can always be ready to cook country. And remember—keep high-quality products on hand, such as fresh herbs and spices, fresh vegetables, fresh country eggs, and the freshest of dairy and meats. High-quality foods will yield the best taste and always reward the cook with the best results.

Let me make the following suggestions for the best stocked country cupboard!

- **Flour:** For breading, baking and making gravies, use a good brand of flour, such as Gold Medal or Pillsbury. Keep both bread flour and all-purpose on hand at all times.

- **Cornmeal:** No country cook can ever be without cornmeal. I love to use Bob's Red Mill medium grind cornmeal for my **Sweet Southern Cornbread,** and a good self-rising yellow or white cornmeal, such as Martha White for battering fish.

- **Baking Powder:** Always check the expiration for the best results; it never hurts to have a fresh box on hand. It would be a shame for those buttermilk biscuits not to rise to their fullest.

- **Baking Soda:** This staple is often overlooked, but like the baking powder, it too can go flat. Again, watch the expiration date, and stock up often. Baking soda activates buttermilk in many recipes.

- **Milk:** Whenever a recipe calls for milk, always use a good whole milk for a richer, smoother taste.

- **Buttermilk:** Many recipes in this cookbook will call for buttermilk as a marinade, such as in the **Southern Fried Chicken.** And always keep it on hand for the **Old-Fashioned Buttermilk Pie.**

- **Butter:** There is just no substitute for real butter. Nothing cooks, bakes, or stirs in like real, creamy rich butter.

- **Eggs:** Use fresh country eggs at room temperature for the best results in your recipe.

- **Fresh Herbs and Spices:** Keep fresh herbs on hand in the summer, such as parsley, thyme, and rosemary, and use up-to-date dried herbs in the winter. Keep cinnamon, ginger, nutmeg, and cloves always on hand. And by all means, use pure vanilla.

- **Lawry's Garlic Salt** coarse ground with **Parsley:** This is my signature spice, and I love to use it on beef, pork, chicken, or fish before preparing the dish. A great boost of flavor.

*(**Rosalie's Cupboard** . . . continued on page 14)*

13

Rosalie Serving Country

(Rosalie's Cupboard . . . continued from page 13)

- **Canola, Olive Oil and Vegetable Shortening:** Fry foods in a good oil for the best taste. Use vegetable shortening, such as Crisco to fry chicken for a crusty golden crust. Use a mild olive oil in cakes rather than vegetable oil; you will love the results, especially in the **Pineapple Upside-Down Cake.**

- **Pecans, Walnuts and Peanuts:** Country folks and southerners alike love their nuts. Bake with them, sugar and toast them in the skillet, add them to stuffing in rolled meat roasts such as the **Pork Loin Roast with Apricots,** or eat them like candy as in the recipe **Candied Nuts.**

- **Meat, Fish and Chicken:** Purchase good fresh cuts of meats, poultry and fish within two to three days of preparing. For best result, use meats, chicken, and fish before freezing.

APPETIZERS and
BEVERAGES

Spending the summers with my older sister and her family when I was only ten years old had a lasting effect on me. My parents lived in Jennings, Missouri, a St. Louis metropolitan suburb, but my older sister lived in the small country town of Rolla, Missouri. Her husband attended the famous Rolla School of Mines University while in college and it was always a treat to visit her.

Her home was an old country farmhouse which they rented, and for a reduced rent they also had the responsibility of caring for the pasture land and a few of the farm animals. During my summer stays, I can remember tagging along with my sister to visit the neighbor folks. If it was evening, they would be in rocking chairs on their front porches, sipping sweet tea and snacking on nuts or fresh fruit, such as apples, peaches, and pears from nearby orchards.

They always acted like it was an honor to have a nearby neighbor pay them a visit, and their hospitality was second to none. "Come on up on the porch," they would say, "and stay a while." Out would come the **Candied Nuts,** some **Brie and Fruit**, or the **Apple Fritters** they had left over from breakfast. Glasses were filled with **Sweet Tea,** or their wonderful **Country Home-made Lemonade.**

While the children were playing jump rope out in the road, the adults would visit with one another on the porch and laugh with such contagious hardiness, anyone left in the house was soon outside to get into the action.

The sunsets were beautiful, and the appetizers and beverages lulled us into a serene setting that took us away from any possible trouble or stress.

It is true that people today are much too scheduled to even know who their neighbors are. Our lives are so filled with coming and going that the front porches are hardly used. Maybe we all need a little "country" put back into our lives—where kids can actually jump rope and adults can sip tea and laugh about the silliest things. Life is just too short not to enjoy the simple things.

So, the next time you decide to invite someone over for supper, as the country folks call it, how about including some down time and just hang out on the porch for a few minutes to enjoy one another, and wind down from the day's events. There may even be a beautiful sunset for your pleasure. "Pass the nuts, and oh, another glass of tea, please."

Crab Balls

Note: *These little crab hors d'oeuvres are addictive. If you like cream cheese and crab meat, you will love these.*

1 (6-ounce) can crabmeat, drained

1 (8-ounce) package cream cheese, softened
1 teaspoon chives, chopped
2 teaspoons green onions, finely chopped
1 teaspoon Lawry's coarse garlic salt
1 teaspoon Worcestershire sauce

½ cup pecans, finely chopped

1. Drain crab meat and place in medium bowl; set aside.

2. Blend the softened cream cheese with the chives, green onion, garlic salt, and Worcestershire sauce. Fold in the crab meat. Shape into small balls. Roll in pecans and spear with colored party toothpicks. Arrange on platter and serve with fresh vegetables. Makes 2 dozen balls.

Crescent Wrapped Brie

Note: *This is an elegant appetizer and is very good served right out of the oven with your choice of fresh fruit, chutney, or fruit preserves. No need to remove the rind over the cheese—this will only add to the flavor. You can even take a little brown sugar mixed with butter and nuts and sprinkle over the top of the cheese before you wrap it in the dough.*

1 (8-ounce) can Pillsbury refrigerated crescent dinner rolls
1 (8-ounce) round Brie Cheese

⅓ cup brown sugar
¼ cup whole pecans,
2 tablespoons butter, cut in small pieces

1 egg, beaten

decorative cutouts
fruit preserves of your choice

1. Preheat oven to 350 degrees. Unroll crescent roll dough and separate at the seam, dividing into two sections. Press and seal the perforations. Place the round of Brie in center of one of the dough squares. Using a leaf or other decorative cutout, cut one shape from each corner of the dough; set aside.

2. Mix the brown sugar, pecans, and butter in a small bowl; place on top of the round of Brie. Place the remaining square of dough on top of the cheese round topped with the brown sugar mixture. Press dough evenly around cheese; fold bottom edges over top edges. Gently stretch dough evenly around cheese and press to seal completely. Brush top with beaten egg. Top with cutouts; brush with beaten egg.

3. Bake 25 to 30 minutes or until golden brown. Cool 15 minutes and serve warm. Cut into small wedges and serve as is or with any fruit preserves. Serves 8 to 10.

Christmas Cheese Ball

Note: *Most everyone loves a party cheese ball during the holidays and this one is very tasty, especially with the pineapple and pecan. Spread it over warm crescents or on your favorite crackers and enjoy the tradition.*

2 (8-ounce) packages cream cheese, softened

1 cup shredded sharp Cheddar cheese

1 tablespoon grated onion

2 tablespoons green pepper, finely chopped

1 (8-ounce) can crushed pineapple, drained

2 teaspoons maraschino cherries,
   finely chopped

½ teaspoon seasoned salt

1 teaspoon lemon juice

1 cup chopped pecans

maraschino cherries

1. Combine softened cream cheese and Cheddar cheese, mixing until well blended. Add onion, green pepper, pineapple, cherries, seasoned salt, and lemon juice.

2. Shape into a ball and roll in chopped pecans. Serve on a cheese platter and garnish with maraschino cherries. Serves 12.

Candied Nuts

Note: *When people look for an appetizer at any gala event, you can be sure they will find the nuts. No matter what is served, folks will be holding a handful of nuts and munching. It is the ever-popular appetizer before dinner. I came across this recipe on a website demonstrated by Veronica Ceczi. Absolutely addictive!*

1 egg white, beaten

1 cup walnuts
1½ cups pecans
1 cup almonds

¾ cup sugar
1 teaspoon cinnamon
¼ teaspoon salt
1 teaspoon vanilla

cooking spray

1. Preheat the oven to 250 degrees. In a medium bowl, beat the egg white just until frothy. Add the walnuts, pecans, and almonds.

2. Add the sugar, cinnamon, salt, and vanilla. Stir the nuts and sugar mixture until well blended and the nuts are thoroughly coated.

3. Spray a cookie sheet with cooking spray and pour the nuts onto the sheet. Spread out with a spoon. Bake in oven for 45 minutes, turning with a fork or spatula every 15 minutes. Remove from oven and let cool on pan. Remove to candy bowl and serve. Makes 3½ cups candied nuts.

(Time: 10 Minutes)

Pineapple Fruit Dip

Note: *Fruit dips are great for dipping fresh fruits in the summer, or with crisp canned fruit at other times of the year. This recipe is light and delicious and so simple to whip up. Sprinkle fresh apples and peaches with lemon juice to avoid turning brown.*

1 small package instant vanilla pudding mix

½ cup sour cream

½ cup milk

1 (8-ounce) can crushed pineapple with juice

lemon juice for sprinkling fruit, as needed

1 strawberry for garnish

1. In medium bowl, blend pudding and sour cream, mixing in milk a little at a time to prevent lumps.

2. When mixture is smooth, fold in the pineapple, including juice. Refrigerate at least 30 minutes to firm mixture. Serve in small bowl placed in center of tray surrounded with sliced fruit, such as sliced apples, strawberries, fresh pineapple chunks, fresh peach slices, or any fruit of your choice. Spear the fruit with toothpicks. Place strawberry in middle of dip. Makes 2½ cups.

(Time: 10 Minutes)

Marshmallow Fruit Dip

Note: *Another great sweet dip for fruits and even some vegetables such as raisin-stuffed celery. It is always a popular and dependable appetizer.*

1 (8-ounce) package cream cheese

1 (7-ounce) jar marshmallow cream

1 tablespoon orange juice

1 teaspoon grated orange peel

1. Mix the cream cheese, marshmallow cream, orange juice, and orange peel in a food processor or electric mixer until blended and smooth. Serve with your favorite fruits or vegetables. Makes 2 cups.

Fried Zucchini Spears

Note: *This is an appetizer that will delight the body and soul and is absolutely wonderful. If you like zucchini, you will love this recipe.*

1 medium large zucchini

3 eggs, beaten

1 cup plain bread crumbs

½ cup grated Parmesan cheese

2 cloves garlic, finely chopped

2 tablespoons fresh parsley, chopped

1 teaspoon salt

¼ teaspoon ground black pepper

½ cup mild olive oil for frying,
   plus more if needed

salt and pepper

Parmesan cheese

1. Cut ends off zucchini and leave skin intact. Cut zucchini into 1 by 3-inch spears. Pierce spears with fork 3 to 4 times. Place eggs in shallow bowl and beat until frothy.

2. Prepare breading by mixing together bread crumbs, cheese, garlic, parsley, salt, and pepper. Place crumb mixture in a gallon zip-lock bag and shake.

3. Dip 2 or 3 zucchini spears into egg mixture and then drop into bread crumb bag. Shake spears until well coated. If more crusty coating is desired, double dip spears back into egg and bread crumbs.

4. In large heavy skillet, heat oil to medium-high heat. Drop spears into hot oil and fry 3 to 4 minutes, turning with fork until golden brown and tender. Adjust heat if oil gets too hot, be careful not to burn. Sprinkle with a little salt and pepper while frying. Remove the zucchini spears to a baking pan lined with paper towels. Sprinkle with Parmesan cheese while hot and serve on platter. Makes about 20 to 25 zucchini spears.

(Time: 15 Minutes)

Battered Fried Mushrooms

Note: *I discovered this appetizer years ago when I had some left-over pancake batter. Having bought mushrooms earlier that day, I decided to dip the mushrooms into the pancake batter and fry them up in oil. We had company and it seemed I couldn't make them fast enough, because everyone was enjoying them so much. A simple and tasty appetizer, these dipped mushrooms are great!*

1 cup Bisquick Baking Mix

⅓ cup milk, plus more if needed

1 egg

1 (8-ounce) package small white
   button mushrooms

Canola or mild olive oil

salt and pepper

1. In large bowl, combine the Bisquick, milk, and egg. Stir until well blended, adding a little more milk if you desire a thinner batter.

2. Wash mushrooms gently under cool water and dry with a paper towel. Remove hard part of stem, leaving a portion of the softer stem. If mushrooms are too large, cut in half. In a heavy 3-quart pot, heat 3 inches of oil over medium high heat. Using a slotted spoon, dip the mushrooms into the pancake batter and let excess batter drain through spoon. Drop the covered mushrooms into the hot oil and fry on both sides until golden. Remove and sprinkle lightly with salt and pepper.

3. Drain mushrooms on paper towels and serve hot. Makes about 15 to 20 mushrooms.

Banana Fruit Punch

Note: *This punch is delicious and when served slushy, leaves a lasting impression. It requires a little time to make, but is very rewarding in the end. It serves a large crowd at bridal showers, special gatherings, or even at Christmas.*

2 cups sugar

2 cups water

1 (12-ounce) can frozen lemonade concentrate

1 (12-ounce) can frozen orange
   juice concentrate

1 (46-ounce) pineapple juice

1 (16-ounce) can crushed pineapple

5 ripe bananas, mashed

2 quarts ginger ale

1 carton of lime or rainbow sherbet

1. In 3-quart heavy pot, bring the sugar and water to a boil and boil for 3 minutes, then cool.

2. Pour sugar water into a large mixing bowl. Prepare the frozen juices according to can directions and add to sugar water, then add the pineapple juice, and crushed pineapple. Mash the bananas well and add to mixture, stirring with a large slotted spoon until thoroughly blended.

3. Pour punch mixture into a 5-gallon ice cream container; cover and freeze 12 to 15 hours. Thaw 2 to 4 hours before serving; punch should be served slushy. Pour into large punch bowl and add ginger ale.

4. Garnish with sherbet using a small ice cream scoop for balls. Makes 50 punch cups.

Cappuccino Punch

Note: *This punch has been the talk of the town ever since its discovery. This rich, smooth, coffee-laced chocolate is so good you will be hooked in no time. This recipe was found on Tea-licious Recipes and comes from Laquita Mullings in Bakersville, California. Prepare larger amounts for parties and showers. Since my dog's name is "Cappuccino," the photographer's assistant, Sonia, thought he should be in the picture. He was extremely agreeable!*

¼ cup instant coffee

½ cup sugar

1 cup boiling water

2 quarts milk

1 quart chocolate ice cream

1 quart vanilla ice cream

Whipped cream for garnish

Cinnamon sugar to sprinkle for garnish, optional

1. Dissolve coffee and sugar in 1 cup boiling water. Place in large punch bowl

2. Add the milk, chocolate ice cream and vanilla ice cream; stir together until blended.

3. Ladle into punch cups and top with whipped cream. Sprinkle cinnamon sugar over whipped cream. Makes 1 gallon.

*M*iss Aimee B's Lemonade

Note: *This lemonade is a famous specialty at Miss Aimee B's Tea Room located in St. Charles, Missouri. It is made with milk and the lemonade offers a sweet/tart taste that is very delicious. Almost everyone that visits the tea room orders the lemonade made with milk.*

2 medium lemons

1½ cups sugar

2 cups milk

1 large container club soda

crushed ice

lemon wedges

1. Wash the lemons; remove ends and quarter them. Hand squeeze the juice from the lemons into a bowl. In either a blender or food processor, coarsely chop the lemons. **DO NOT PUREE!** Add the coarsely chopped lemons to the bowl.

2. Add the sugar and stir well. Let the mixture sit for 30 minutes to allow the sugar to pull the juices out of the lemons. Add the milk and stir again. Cover and refrigerate several hours or overnight.

3. To serve, strain the concentrate to remove the rinds and seeds. Fill a glass with ½ cup lemonade mixture, ½ cup club soda, and ½ cup crushed ice. Stir well and serve with a lemon wedge for garnish. Serves 6. To make this for a crowd, use 11 lemons, 8 cups sugar, and 11 cups milk. Serves 32.

Alexandra & Reagan Harpole

Rosalie Serving Country

The LEMONADE STAND

The month of July can deliver some very hot sultry days, and between storms and rain clouds, one can experience the "dog days" of summer. I guess that was when the pets stayed outside and hid under the porch to cool off…way back when we didn't have air conditioning. We mostly had fans, left all the windows open, played hopscotch on the sidewalks, and drank lemonade. Life was a blast way back in the 1950's,—with *Howdy Dowdy, Kukla, Fran and Ollie,* and of course *Annette Funnicello.* What more could a kid ask for?

What would life be without all these sweet memories? Kids playing out in the street while our moms and dads sat visiting with the neighbors up on the front porches. It was during those very hot days when kids were home from school, and moms either worked very little or were mostly at home, that we got the idea to make a lemonade stand. We would get out the little card table, cover it with a white tablecloth and ask mom to help us make the famous sign, "Lemonade For Sale, 10 cents a cup." I can remember her using real lemons and filling up a gallon jar with the sweet mixture topped with ice. "Now, I'm not going to all this trouble if you kids don't stay out there all afternoon. Once you have your sign up, you need to stick with it," she said.

So, there we were, my friends and I, at the end of the driveway flagging down cars. We were committed! One friend would pour the lemonade while I would collect the money. Our mason jar was jingling with nickels and dimes, and every now and then someone would give us a quarter. If the sun was beating down, we didn't notice, since we were drinking as much lemonade as we were selling. We couldn't have been happier! After two straight days of the **"LEMONADE STAND,"** we decided we had enough money—and besides, we couldn't miss the *Mouseketeers* two days in a row.

After growing up and having a family of my own, I recalled a very hot day in July when I decided to make the kids a big gallon jar of lemonade. We were out on the front porch when Scott said, "Wow, we could have a lemonade stand and sell it down by the driveway. Jeff, you get Dad to make us a sign and Mom can make some more lemonade." Funny how I remember telling the boys, "Now, I'm not going to all this trouble if you kids don't stay out there all afternoon; you can't be changing your mind, even though it is very hot!" They had fun, gave their friends free samples, and most of all made a lifetime memory.

I write about this because I have been trying to make real country lemonade to put in my book *Rosalie Serving Country.* After a couple of tries, I decided the best way was to make a syrup of boiling water and sugar and then add the lemon juice. Wow! It was wonderful! The only difference was lemons were two for five cents the day my mom made up her lemonade, compared to sixty cents a lemon this past week. But, in both cases the memories are still as vivid as ever.

The moral? Make a memory with your children or grandchildren! Pick a day that you can spend with them and let them experience the lemonade stand. You both will have a blast!

27

Country Homemade Lemonade

Note: *There is just no substitute for homemade lemonade to quench thirst in the summertime. The trick is to dissolve the sugar in hot water to make a thin syrup before adding the lemon juice. This always makes the best lemonade. Make in any amount by remembering these simple measurements; 1 cup sugar, 1 cup water, 1 cup lemon juice, and 3 to 4 cups cold water.*

1 cup sugar

1 cup water

1 cup freshly squeezed lemon juice, seeds extracted

1 tablespoon freshly grated lemon rind

3 to 4 cups cold water

lemon and lime slices

1. In small heavy saucepan, heat the sugar and water until the sugar is completely dissolved or until a thin syrup forms.

2. Use a juicer and extract juice from 4 to 6 lemons, enough for one cup of juice. Add the juice, grated lemon rind, and the sugar water to a pitcher; stir the liquids well. Add the cold water and mix together.

3. Taste, and if a little sweet for your taste, add a little more lemon juice. Serve over crushed ice, garnished with a lemon or lime slice. Makes 1½ quarts and serves 6. Note: Substitute ⅔ cup Splenda for 1 cup sugar for a sugar-free lemonade.

(Time: 15 Minutes)

Good Ol' Alabama Sweet Tea

Note: *This sweet tea is found in houses, churches, and cafes all over the great state of Alabama. It has been said that it is the best sweet tea ever! Fresh-squeezed lemon, lime, or even orange juice can be added for an extra flavor. Be sure to use a good tasting water for the best results. This recipe was submitted by **LOVECATS 2001 for Allrecipes**.*

1 gallon-sized pitcher

2 cups sugar

2 quarts water

1 tray or 2 cups ice cubes

3 family sized teabags orange pekoe tea

3 cups cold water

¼ cup freshly squeezed lemon, lime, or orange juice, optional

1. Pour the sugar into a large pitcher. Bring 2 quarts water to a boil in a large heavy pot. When the water begins to boil, remove from heat and add the teabags. Let teabags steep in the water for 5 to 6 minutes.

2. Remove the tea bags and return pot with tea to the heat. Bring just to a boil, and then pour into the pitcher. Stir until the sugar is dissolved. Add ice and stir until most of it melts. Fill the pitcher the rest of the way with cold water and stir until blended. Serves 16.

Peach Nectar Tea

Note: *Here is another "Tea House" beverage. This one is an anytime treat, but especially great around the holidays and those cold nights. Serve it warm or cold as a perfect beverage for your daytime or evening parties.*

8 cups water, divided
2 family-sized tea bags

¾ cup sugar, or ⅔ cup Splenda
1 (5.5 ounce) can Kern's Peach
   Nectar Juice

Peach slices for garnish, optional

1. Brew tea in 6 cups water using coffee or tea maker. Let steep for 8 to 10 minutes. Remove tea bags, and pour tea into a pitcher while still very hot.

2. Add the sugar or Splenda and the peach nectar. Add 2 cups remaining water and stir together. Taste for your desired sweetness, adding more sugar as needed. Makes 2¼ quarts.

29

White Grape Raspberry Tea

Note: *This raspberry tea is one of the best I have ever experienced. I created it one day after trying several recipes and decided I liked it the best. Wonderful served warm on a cold night or over crushed ice on a warm day. Garnish with frozen raspberries, if desired.*

12 cups water

4 family size tea bags

1 cup sugar or ⅔ cup Splenda

¼ cup freshly-squeezed lemon juice

1 (11.5 ounce) Welch's White Grape Raspberry
frozen juice concentrate

1 can water

fresh frozen raspberries

1. In large pot, bring 12 cups water to a boil. Add the tea bags and steep in water 8 to 10 minutes, until tea is a deep dark color.

2. Add the sugar or Splenda and stir well to dissolve; stir in lemon juice. Next, add the frozen white grape raspberry juice, plus 1 can water. Stir the mixture well until flavors are combined. Taste, adding more sugar if desired.

3. Serve the tea warm or iced and garnish with 3 to 4 fresh frozen raspberries. Makes almost 1 gallon of tea.

Sugar-free Raspberry Zinger Tea

Note: *This tea is so delicious, you will never know it is sugar free. My husband who is a diabetic, can drink to his heart's desire and feel like he is at a high-priced restaurant. I'm sure you will love it, too.*

8 cups water, divided

2 family size tea bags

4 Celestial Seasoning Raspberry Zinger tea packets

¾ cup Splenda

1 tablespoon lemon juice

2 cups fresh frozen raspberries

mint leaves

1. Brew tea in 6 cups water using coffee or tea maker. Let steep for 8 to 10 minutes. Remove tea bags, and pour hot tea into a large pitcher.

2. Add the Splenda, lemon juice, and 1 to 2 cups water, depending on taste. Add the 2 cups fresh frozen raspberries. Let the tea sit for several minutes, stirring often to blend raspberry flavor. Strain tea through strainer, using a spoon to squeeze some of the raspberry pulp back into the tea.

3. Serve warm or over crushed ice and garnish with mint leaves. Makes 2½ quarts tea.

Rosalie Serving Country

Homemade Eggnog

Note: *Homemade Eggnog is easy to make and so good during the Thanksgiving and Christmas holidays. This recipe has a milkshake taste and is very creamy. Served cold from a pretty punch bowl and sprinkled with nutmeg, this drink will bring cheer and goodness to your family and friends.*

6 eggs, separated

¾ cup sugar

½ teaspoon vanilla

¼ teaspoon ground nutmeg

2 teaspoons rum extract

3 cups heavy whipping cream

2 cups whole milk

6 egg whites

¼ cup sugar

ground nutmeg

1. Beat egg yolks with electric mixer until thick and lemon colored; gradually add sugar, **vanilla**, nutmeg, and rum extract. Stir in cream and milk and beat until frothy. Pour eggnog **mixture** into a covered pitcher and chill for 6 to 8 hours to bring out the flavor. Place egg whites **in a** covered container and leave at room temperature until ready to use.

2. Remove eggnog from refrigerator and pour into a punch bowl.

3. Transfer egg whites to a large mixing bowl and using electric mixer, beat whites until soft peaks form. Add sugar and continue to beat until stiff. Fold egg whites into the chilled eggnog mixture until thoroughly blended. Sprinkle nutmeg lightly over the top of the **eggnog** and ladle into small cups. Makes about 2½ quarts.

BREAKFAST
BISCUITS and
COFFEE CAKES

A BREAKFAST TO REMEMBER

I grew up with a mom who loved to cook breakfast, especially on Sunday morning right after we returned from church. My father, being the butcher, always made sure Mom had plenty of breakfast steaks, thick sliced bacon, and his Italian Salsiccia. She would make scrambled eggs and toast her leftover homemade bread. He loved his "peanut cake," as he called it, for his "sweet." By the time lunch came around, we were still full. I thought no one could top my mother for breakfast.

Moving to Troy, Missouri, the rural life of pastures, livestock, and gravel roads was a little dramatic for the city girl that I was. I was the young mother of three who went to the mall for therapy. I thought life would be much slower in the country setting, but I soon found out differently, especially for those who made farming their living.

Not long after the church in Troy voted my husband in as their pastor, the church ladies were very excited to do their breakfast fund raiser. They called it *"Country Sausage and Eggs Breakfast."* Everyone seemed to get involved, and each one used their specific talents to make it successful. One of the farmers donated a whole hog for the sausage, and the ladies fixed the breakfast.

I remember going downstairs to the fellowship hall after Sunday service and smelling the **Buttermilk Biscuits** that Mildred Cox was getting out of the oven. She loved to make her biscuits, and no one dared compete. Another lady, Ann Lavy, was stirring a large cast iron skillet full of the **Country Milk Sausage Gravy.** There were big platters of fluffy scrambled eggs, sausage, and the most wonderful **Fried Potatoes & Onions.** Bowls were filled with the warm biscuits, along with plenty of homemade **Oven Apple Butter,** fresh made jellies, and real butter. Mildred had even made her famous fried pies, much like the **Apple Fritters** which are included in this section.

I will never forget that breakfast, especially the smooth gravy ladled over the open biscuit with chunks of the best sausage I had ever tasted. While I will always cherish my upbringing and my mother's wonderful Italian Cuisine, I must say the experience that I had was a breakfast to remember. I hope you too will cook these wonderful country breakfast meals, all of which are just as great as those I tasted many years ago. Celebrate your family this Sunday, and fix one of these favorites for all to remember. And for a real treat, get up just a little early and surprise them with the **Cinnamon Rolls with Cream Cheese Icing.** You will definitely make a memory and your spouse and children will love you forever.

Rosalie Serving Country

Country Morning Casserole

Note: *This is a great country morning breakfast that's easy and delicious. It can be made the night before, covered and placed in refrigerator; then brought out in the morning and baked. Perfect for guests coming in or just for a family gathering. Serve with **Simple Morning Gravy** recipe found on page 39 and **Whipping Cream Biscuits** recipe found on page 37.*

melted butter

3 cups frozen hash brown potatoes

½ cup green onions, chopped

1 cup fresh mushrooms, sliced (optional)

½ stick butter

2 cups cooked pork sausage, crumbled

10 eggs, beaten

½ cup milk

1 teaspoon salt

½ teaspoon fine ground pepper

2 cups cheddar cheese, shredded

parsley sprigs

strawberries

1 recipe **Simple Morning Gravy,** optional

1. Preheat oven to 350 degrees. Using a 13 by 9-inch deep baking pan, brush about 2 teaspoons butter into bottom and sides of pan. Layer the ingredients, starting with the hash browns on the bottom. Next, sprinkle the onions over the hash browns and add the mushrooms. Cut the butter in small pieces and scatter over the mushrooms.

2. Cook the pork sausage until no longer pink. Drain well and crumble the sausage over the butter and mushrooms. Beat the eggs in a medium bowl until fluffy, about 1 to 2 minutes. Add the milk, salt, and pepper. Continue to beat another few seconds. Pour eggs over the layers, and top with cheddar cheese.

3. Bake casserole for 20 to 25 minutes, or until eggs are set. Check casserole by inserting a butter knife through the middle of the casserole. The knife should come out clean. If still too wet, continue baking another 5 minutes.

4. Remove from oven; cut into squares and serve while warm. Top with gravy if desired and serve with **Whipping Cream Biscuits.** Garnish each place with a parsley sprig and one or two strawberries. Serves 4 to 6.

(Time: 40 Minutes)

Country Skillet Breakfast

Note: *This heavenly breakfast was served to me at Cracker Barrel, and I loved it so much, I came home, wrote the recipe and made it the next day. The skillets can be purchased at Cracker Barrel or can be found at most kitchen specialty shops. If you still can't find the smaller skillet, use a 10½-inch large cast iron and share it for four. When served with the awesome **Buttermilk Biscuits** recipe found on page 37, you will have a bed and breakfast delight!*

4 (6½-inch cast iron skillets)
   or 1 (10½-inch cast iron skillet)

1 **Country Milk Sausage Gravy** recipe
   found on page 38

1 **Buttermilk Biscuits** recipe
found on page 37

2 medium red potatoes, unpeeled and cut
   into 1-inch chunks
3 to 4 tablespoons bacon drippings, plus more
   if needed
1 red bell pepper, cut into 1½-inch strips
1 green bell pepper, cut into 1½-inch strips
1 large onion, cut into small 1-inch chunks

1 teaspoon salt
½ teaspoon ground black pepper

8 eggs, beaten
⅓ cup milk
¼ cup bacon drippings or mild olive oil

2 cups mild shredded cheddar cheese

1. Make the **Country Milk Sausage Gravy** as directed and keep on very low heat, stirring occasionally.

2. Microwave potatoes for 2 to 3 minutes to soften, do not fully cook. Cut potatoes into small chunks. Place potatoes in large skillet with bacon drippings. Turn heat to medium high and add the bell peppers and onion. Season the vegetables with salt and pepper and sauté for 8 to 10 minutes, or until tender. Turn heat to very low to keep warm.

3. While vegetables are sautéing, prepare and bake the **Buttermilk Biscuits.**

4. Combine eggs and milk and beat together until light and foamy. Cook eggs in bacon drippings in another large skillet, scrambling until light and fluffy. Remove quickly and place in bowl.

5. To assemble skillets, divide the vegetables between the four skillets (or one large skillet). Divide the sausage gravy in the same manner and pour over vegetables. Divide eggs equally over gravy. Top with ½ cup shredded cheese. Place skillets in oven under broiler for 30 seconds to melt cheese. Serve with hot biscuits. Makes 4 skillet breakfasts.

Rosalie Serving Country

Creamed Chipped Beef over Toast

Note: *This is an old recipe that was suggested to me from many of the nurses I work with. They said they had it as children growing up, and thought it was a country dish. It is very tasty and needs no salt, since the chipped beef is very salty. An old time favorite revived.*

2 tablespoons butter

½ pound mushrooms, sliced, optional

6 ounces dried chipped beef

1 tablespoon Worcestershire sauce

4 slices sourdough bread, toasted

Cream Sauce

4 tablespoons butter

3 tablespoons flour

1¾ cups milk

pepper

sprinkle of fresh grated or dry nutmeg

1. Melt butter in large heavy skillet. Add the mushrooms and sauté for 1 to 2 minutes. Add the chipped beef and the Worcestershire sauce, and heat until beef is warmed through. Keep on low heat while making the cream sauce.

2. Make the cream sauce by melting the butter in a heavy skillet. Over medium heat, stir in the flour and allow to bubble for 30 seconds, stirring often. Slowly pour in the milk a little at a time, stirring constantly to avoid lumping. Continue to stir until thick and creamy. Stir in pepper to taste and add a little nutmeg.

3. Toast 4 slices sourdough bread. Place 1 piece of toast on plate, top with beef mixture. Pour cream sauce over beef and serve warm. Serves 4.

Buttermilk Biscuits

Note: *These biscuits are light and airy and are always a favorite on the country table. The dough may be a little sticky, but can easily be handled with a metal dough scraper and floured hands. Place them close together for soft sides or 1 inch apart for crusty sides. These biscuits go well with **Country Milk Sausage Gravy** recipe found on page 38.*

2 cups all-purpose flour

1 tablespoon baking powder

1 teaspoon baking soda

½ teaspoon salt

⅓ cup butter, cut into pieces

¾ cup buttermilk

butter for brushing biscuits

1. Preheat oven to 425 degrees. In medium bowl combine flour, baking powder, baking soda, and salt. Mix together well. Cut butter into flour mixture with a pastry blender, or rub between hands until dough resembles small peas.

2. Add buttermilk, stirring just until dry ingredients are moistened.

3. Turn dough onto a lightly floured surface and with metal dough scraper, lift the dough and fold it over on the floured surface; knead 3 or 4 times. Pat or roll dough to a ¾-inch thickness; cut with a 2½-inch round biscuit cutter. Place biscuits on a lightly greased baking pan and arrange as desired.

4. Bake for 10 to 12 minutes. Remove from oven and brush biscuits with melted butter. Makes 8 biscuits.

(Time: 15 Minutes)

Whipping Cream Biscuits

Note: *These biscuits are so simple, my son Scott would whip them up while I made breakfast. They will actually melt in your mouth with goodness.*

2 cups self-rising flour

1¼ cups heavy whipping cream, plus more if needed

butter or jam

1. Preheat oven to 400 degrees. Combine flour and cream, stirring with a fork until blended. The dough may be stiff, but will come together. Turn out onto a lightly floured surface; knead 3 or 4 times. Dust with a little flour beneath dough to avoid sticking and roll dough to a ½ inch thickness. Cut dough with a 2-inch biscuit cutter.

2. Place biscuits, sides touching, on a lightly greased baking sheet and let set for about 5 minutes. The biscuits will rise as they set. Place pan in oven and bake for 10 to 12 minutes. Serve warm with butter and jam. Makes 12 biscuits.

37

(Time: 15 Minutes)

Country Milk Sausage Gravy

Note: *This gravy is simple and rich with flavors of both bacon and sausage, and can be easily doubled for a large crowd. Serve over the* **Whipping Cream Biscuits** *and* **Buttermilk Biscuits** *recipes found on page 37. It is also great with breakfast casseroles or with an evening omelet. Smooth as satin and very filling, it also keeps well in the refrigerator for a day or two.*

1 roll pork sausage, about 2 cups

4 tablespoons bacon drippings

⅓ cup flour

½ teaspoon salt

¼ teaspoon ground black pepper

4 cups whole milk

salt and pepper

1. In large heavy skillet, fry sausage in bacon drippings on medium heat until no longer pink and cooked through.

2. Stir in the flour, salt, and pepper all at once. Slowly add milk 1 cup at a time over medium heat; stir until mixture thickens and is hot and bubbly. For a thicker gravy, use less milk. Boil gently 1 to 2 minutes longer. Add additional salt and pepper to taste. Makes 6 cups gravy.

Fried Potatoes & Onions

Note: *What can say country better than a big skillet of **Fried Potatoes & Onions**? I can remember making pan after pan when working in the kitchen at the Thresher's Country Fair in Elsberry, Missouri. It started out as a breakfast item, but because it was so popular, it was served at every meal. Fried up crunchy yet tender, these are the best!*

3 to 4 large red or brown potatoes, unpeeled

1 medium onion

salt and pepper

½ cup bacon drippings or Canola oil

1. Wash potatoes and pat dry. Cut potatoes in half lengthwise and then in half again. Slice into ¼-inch slices. Cut onion in half and into slices.

2. Fry potatoes and onions in hot oil in a 10-inch cast-iron skillet over medium-high heat 10 to 12 minutes, stirring often. Sprinkle with salt and pepper to taste while potatoes are frying. After potatoes are browned, lower heat and cover.

3. When potatoes are crusty brown and soft, remove to a large platter and serve warm. Serves 6 to 8.

(Time: 10 Minutes)

Simple Morning Gravy

Note: *This gravy is simple milk gravy made with butter instead of bacon or sausage drippings. A great substitute when you want good gravy, but have no meat drippings. Delicious and smooth, it is good to have on hand to ladle over potatoes, omelets, or to serve over **Country Morning Casserole** recipe found on page 33.*

3 tablespoons butter

2 tablespoons flour

salt and pepper

dash of red pepper

2 to 2½ cups milk

1. Place butter in skillet, and heat until bubbly and golden brown, about 1 minute. Add the flour all at once. Stirring constantly, melt flour into butter until mixture is smooth.

2. Slowly add milk 1 cup at a time over medium heat, stirring until mixture bubbles. Continue to add milk until desired thickness is reached. Turn heat down and add the salt, pepper and red pepper to taste. Gravy will continue to thicken as it simmers. Makes about 2½ cups gravy.

(Time: 5 Hours)

Oven Apple Butter

Note: *This apple butter is great on biscuits, toast, and even used in cakes. Mostly unattended, you can make it on your day off and the results will long be remembered.*

8 Granny Smith apples, cored, peeled, and diced

1 cup apple juice

1 cup sugar

1 teaspoon cinnamon

butter

1. Preheat oven to 275 degrees. Using a Dutch oven, cook apples and juice over medium heat for 30 minutes or until apples are tender. Mash apples with a potato masher and stir well.

2. Stir in the sugar and cinnamon. Pour apple mixture into a butter-coated oven-proof 11 by 7-inch baking dish.

3. Bake uncovered for 4½ hours, stirring every hour, or until reaching spreading consistency. Cool and pour into 1-cup fruit jars; seal with lid. Refrigerate and use as desired. Makes 3 cups.

Apple Fritters

Note: *Great on the breakfast buffet, these sweet old-fashioned apple fritters will disappear in no time. Sprinkled with lots of powdered sugar and served while still warm or slightly cooled, they are much like a cake donut. Three dozen too many? Cut the recipe in half—it works just as well.*

3 cups all-purpose flour

½ teaspoon salt

2 teaspoons baking powder

½ cup sugar

1 large egg

1 cup milk

¼ cup butter, melted

2 teaspoon grated orange rind

¼ cup fresh orange juice

2 cups apples finely chopped

1 teaspoon vanilla extract

mild olive oil

sifted powdered sugar

1. Combine the flour, salt, baking powder and sugar in large bowl; mix together.

2. In a separate bowl, combine the egg, milk, and butter and beat together lightly. Stir in the orange rind, orange juice, apples, and vanilla extract. Add to flour mixture and stir together just until dry ingredients are moistened.

3. Pour oil to a depth of 2 to 3-inches into a large Dutch oven; heat to 350 degrees. Drop batter by rounded tablespoons into hot oil. Fry fritters in batches for 1½ minutes on each side or until golden. Drain fritters well on paper towels and cool slightly. Sprinkle with powdered sugar. Makes 3 dozen.

(Time: 20 Minutes)

uttermilk Pancakes

Note: *These pancakes are a little more work than a mix, but definitely worth the time. Make them while your husband and kids are asleep; they will quickly awake when they smell the aroma. They are very light and they taste great.*

1 ⅔ cups buttermilk
1 teaspoon baking soda

3 egg yolks, beaten
¼ cup melted butter
1 teaspoon vanilla

1½ cups all-purpose flour
1 teaspoon baking powder
½ teaspoon salt
1 teaspoon sugar

3 egg whites

vegetable oil or mild olive oil

1 cup pecans
2 tablespoons sugar

1. Pour buttermilk into a 2-cup bowl and add the baking soda, mixing with a fork to dissolve. Let stand for about 5 minutes. Beat the egg yolks until fluffy and add the butter and vanilla. Add the buttermilk mixture to the egg yolk mixture and whisk together well.

2. Mix the flour, baking powder, salt, and sugar in a large bowl. Slowly add the wet ingredients to the dry ingredients; mixing together until smooth.

3. Beat the egg whites until stiff and fold into the batter. Let batter stand 5 minutes.

4. In lightly oiled skillet, over medium-high heat, pour ¼ cup batter and fry on one side until bubbles appear on surface, then turn and fry on the other side until golden brown.

5. Place pecans in dry skillet and add the sugar. Stir constantly over medium heat until pecans are toasted and become aromatic, about 3 minutes. Serve 3 pancakes on a plate and garnish with sugar coated pecans if desired. Use syrup or topping of your choice. Makes about 12 large, or 24 small pancakes.

Wheat Pancakes with Oats & Pecans

Note: *These guilt-free pancakes will melt in your mouth. Low in fat and high in fiber, you can eat this breakfast often and love every bite. They start out like buttermilk pancakes, but take a twist in the middle of the recipe. Top with butter pecan syrup; your family will be hooked.*

2 cups buttermilk

1 teaspoon baking soda

2 egg yolks, beaten

¼ cup melted butter

½ teaspoon butter extract

1 teaspoon vanilla extract

1¼ cups Bob's Red Mill whole wheat flour

¼ cup all-purpose flour

¼ cup brown sugar

⅓ cup old-fashioned oats

⅓ cup chopped pecans

1 teaspoon baking powder

½ teaspoon salt

3 egg whites

mild olive oil

syrup

1. Pour buttermilk into a 2-cup measuring cup and add the baking soda, mixing with a fork to dissolve. Let stand for about 5 minutes.

2. In a large bowl, beat the egg yolks until fluffy; add the melted butter, butter extract, and vanilla extract. Add the buttermilk mixture to the egg yolk mixture and whisk together well.

3. Mix the flours, brown sugar, oats, pecans, baking powder, and salt. Slowly add the wet ingredients to the dry ingredients, mixing together until smooth.

4. Beat the egg whites until stiff and fold into the batter. Let batter stand 5 minutes.

5. In lightly oiled skillet, pour in ¼ cup batter and turn heat to medium-high. Do not crowd pancakes. Fry on one side until bubbles appear on surface; turn and fry on the other side until golden brown. If pancakes darken too quickly, lower heat.

6. Serve 3 pancakes on a plate and top with butter pecan or maple syrup. Makes 12 (4-inch) pancakes.

Blueberry Muffins

est Blueberry Muffins

Note: *These crunchy-on-top warm blueberry muffins are just what you've desired. Made with sweet butter and sour cream, they are wonderful. Serve them right out of the oven covered with crunchy sweet streusel topping and coupled with a cup of your favorite coffee. You are sure to forget your troubles.*

1 cup sugar

½ cup butter

2 eggs

1 teaspoon vanilla

2 cups all-purpose flour

1 teaspoon baking powder

1 teaspoon baking soda

½ teaspoon salt

1 (8-ounce) carton sour cream

1 pint fresh blueberries

melted butter

flour

Streusel Topping

¾ cup flour

¾ cup sugar

½ cup butter

1. Preheat oven to 350 degrees. Cream butter and gradually add sugar, beating at medium speed with electric mixer. Add eggs one at a time, beating after each addition. Stir in vanilla.

2. Combine flour, baking powder, baking soda, and salt; add to creamed mixture alternately with sour cream, beginning and ending with flour mixture.

3. Wash blueberries under cool water; pat dry with paper towel. Gently fold blueberries into batter; batter will be a little stiff.

4. Use a regular 12-cup and a regular 6-cup muffin pan for small muffins, or two giant 6-cup muffin pans to make 8 giant muffins. Coat pans with butter and dust with flour, or use muffin liners.

5. Prepare the streusel topping. Using a pastry blender or your hands, combine the flour, sugar and butter until mixture becomes crumbly.

6. Fill the muffin cups ⅔ full with batter and top with 3 to 4 tablespoons streusel. Bake for 25 to 28 minutes, or until firm and golden brown. Serve warm with butter. Makes 1½ dozen small muffins or 6 to 8 giant muffins.

Cinnamon Rolls
with Cream Cheese Icing

Rosalie Serving Country

Cinnamon Rolls with Cream Cheese Icing

Note: These cinnamon rolls could very well be a clone for the famous Cinnabon. They are so good and easy, especially if you have a bread machine. If not, then knead the dough as you would for bread. A delicious breakfast item or anytime dessert, you will be very pleased with this recipe and the heavenly scent that will fill your kitchen.

4½ cups bread flour

1 teaspoon salt

½ cup granulated sugar

1 cup warm whole milk, 110 to 115 degrees

2½ teaspoons yeast

2 eggs beaten, room temperature

⅓ cup butter, melted

1 to 2 tablespoons melted butter

Filling

1 cup brown sugar

2½ tablespoons cinnamon

⅓ cup butter, melted

cooking spray

Icing

1 (3-ounce) package cream cheese, softened

¼ cup butter, softened

1½ cups powdered sugar

½ teaspoon vanilla

1. Preheat oven to 350 degrees. If using a bread machine, place the first seven ingredients in the machine and set to bread instruction. Let the dough double in size, then punch down and let rest on counter 10 minutes. If kneading the bread by hand, place the flour, salt and sugar in a large bowl. Add the yeast to the warm milk and let stand for 8 minutes to foam up yeast. Make a well in the middle of the flour and add the yeast milk, eggs, and warm butter in the center. Gently bring the flour into the egg mixture a little at a time and work the mixture together until the dough forms a ball. Knead the dough about 8 minutes, or until the dough feels elastic. Keep dough in same bowl and pour butter over the top. Roll dough over to coat with butter and cover with a towel. Keep in warm place until doubled in size, about 1 to 1½ hours. Punch dough down and let rest on counter 10 minutes.

2. In small bowl make the filling by combining the brown sugar and cinnamon; mix together and set aside.

3. On a floured counter, roll dough to a 16 by 21-inch rectangle, turning once or twice to avoid sticking and dusting lightly with flour as needed. Spread the melted butter over the dough with a spatula. Sprinkle the butter with the cinnamon sugar. Roll the dough jelly-roll style and cut into 12 slices.

4. Lightly spray a 9 by 13-inch baking pan with cooking spray. Place the rolls in the pan about 1 inch apart and cover with towel. Let the rolls rise until double in size, about 30 to 40 minutes. Place in oven and bake for 30 minutes. Remove and let cool slightly.

5. Prepare icing by beating the cream cheese, butter, powdered sugar, and vanilla together until smooth. Spread over warm rolls and serve. Makes 1 dozen cinnamon rolls.

Cinnamon Sugar Coffee Cake

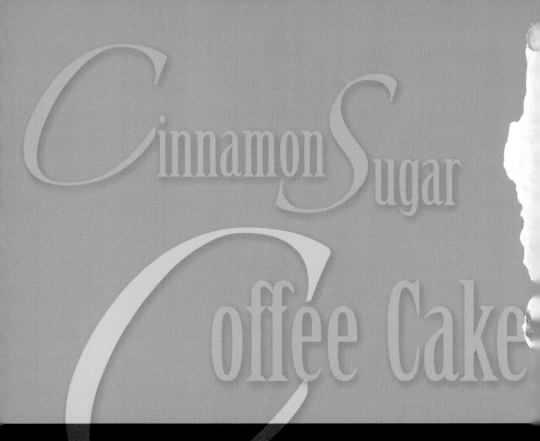

Rosalie Serving Country

innamon Sugar Coffee Cake

Note: *This mouthful of bliss comes from a dear lady, Madeline Richmond, who lives in Sandstone, West Virginia. Her children attend the Terre Haute, Indiana, New Life Church where our son, Jeff, is the pastor. Affectionately known as "Grandma Richmond," she has made this cake for her family for 25 years. I was so blessed to be served a piece while visiting one Sunday and as soon as it entered my mouth, I knew it must be in my* **Rosalie Serving Country Cookbook.** *Incredibly delicious!*

1 (10-inch) metal Bundt pan
butter
flour

1 Duncan Hines Moist Deluxe
   yellow cake mix
1 (3.4-ounce) box Jell-O instant
   vanilla pudding

¾ cup mild olive oil
¾ cup water
4 eggs
1 teaspoon butter extract
1 teaspoon pure vanilla

Filling
¾ cup sugar
¾ cup walnuts, chopped
7 teaspoons cinnamon

Almond Glaze
1 cup powdered sugar
1 to 2 tablespoons milk
½ teaspoon almond extract

1. Preheat oven to 350 degrees. Butter Bundt pan and dust with flour; set aside. In large bowl stir together cake mix and vanilla pudding.

2. Add the olive oil, water, eggs, butter extract and vanilla. Stir by hand just until ingredients are blended. Pour half the batter in pan.

3. Make the filling by combining the sugar, walnuts, and cinnamon. On top of batter, add half of cinnamon sugar mixture and fold/swirl into cake batter. Add remainder batter and sprinkle the rest of the cinnamon sugar over top. Swirl in some of the sugar mixture, leaving the rest loose on top. Bake for 1 hour. Cake is done when it springs back with light touch to top. Remove from oven and let sit 5 minutes.

4. Loosen cake by running a knife around side of pan. Gently invert onto a pretty cake platter; let cool to slightly warm. Make glaze by combining the powdered sugar, milk, and almond extract. Pour glaze over top and sides of cake. Serve warm or at room temperature. Serves 12.

49

Cherry Pie Coffee Cake

Note: *This coffee cake is wonderful for family or special guests and is very versatile. It can be made with any pie filling—cherry, peach, blueberry or apple. If using apple, add ¼ cup brown sugar and ¼ teaspoon cinnamon to pie filling. Delicious!*

½ cup butter

1 cup sugar

2 eggs

1 teaspoon almond extract

2 cups all-purpose flour

1 teaspoon baking powder

1 teaspoon baking soda

½ teaspoon salt

1 (8-ounce) carton sour cream

1½ (1-pound 5-ounce) cans cherry pie filling

⅓ cup sugar

1 teaspoon almond extract

1 tablespoon butter

Streusel Topping

1 cup flour

¾ cup sugar

½ cup butter

Glaze

¾ cup sifted powdered sugar

½ teaspoon almond extract

1½ tablespoons warm water

1. Preheat oven to 350 degrees. Cream butter and gradually add sugar, beating at medium speed with an electric mixer. Add eggs one at a time, beating after each addition. Stir in almond extract.

2. Combine flour, baking powder, baking soda, and salt; add to creamed mixture alternately with sour cream, beginning and ending with flour mixture.

3. Stir together cherry pie filling, sugar, and almond extract.

4. Coat bottom of 13 by 9-inch pan with butter, then spoon in ¾ of the batter. Spread pie filling over batter. Place dollops of remaining batter over filling.

5. Make streusel topping by combining flour and sugar. Work in the butter until small clumps form. Spread the streusel over the dollops of batter.

6. Bake in oven for 55 minutes to 1 hour. Remove and let cool 5 minutes. Combine glaze ingredients and drizzle over warm cake. Serve warm or at room temperature. Serves 15.

SOUPS and SALADS

I'LL HAVE A CUP OF SOUP AND A SALAD, PLEASE

How many times have we visited our favorite little tea house with friends, studied the menu amid small talk and laughter, and then decided, "I'll have a cup of soup and a salad, please." Is it the comfort in the soup, or the light-heartiness of the salad that prompts us to choose? Well, perhaps both. Everyone loves a good cup or bowl of hearty soup, especially on cold days, and without a doubt, a wonderful salad with a good roll is exactly what pleases the palate.

Soups and salads have long been the "meal before the meal," and for many of us, they were so filling we could have easily ended with a dessert and felt well satisfied. A soul-quenching bowl of piping hot soup like the **Hearty Beef & Vegetable** served with just the right salad such as the **Southern Salad with Strawberry Vinaigrette** is always pleasing.

Another all-time country soup favorite is of course the **First Prize Ham & Bean Soup.** When served with chopped onions and cornbread, one could definitely eat to oblivion. Some of my other favorites are **Broccoli Cheese Soup,** a soup as smooth as satin, and the delicious **Baked Potato Soup,** filled with the goodness of a loaded baked potato. These are recipes your family will long remember as special, and deserve to be kept as family treasures.

Salads are not only diverse, but can be used to complement the main course. For instance the best barbecue would not be complete without my mother, Ann Fiorino's, **Awesome Potato Salad.** Or, how could we get through Thanksgiving dinner without my granddaughter, Taylor's, favorite **Cranberry Raspberry Salad**?

And don't forget two great luncheon salads to serve with sweet tea or lemonade: **Crunchy Chicken Salad** and the wonderful **Waldorf Salad.** Get together with family and friends, and don't forget to say… "I'll have a cup of soup and a salad, please."

Rosalie Serving Country

51

Baked Potato Soup

Rosalie Serving Country

Baked Potato Soup

Note: *Love baked potatoes? Then this is the soup for you. Rich, creamy and chuck full of goodness, you can proudly serve this for any occasion. Everyone will want seconds, and this recipe makes a good amount. Wonderful!*

4 large baking potatoes

12 slices bacon

⅔ cup butter
½ cup flour
5 cups whole milk
1 cup Kitchen Basics low-sodium
   chicken broth
½ teaspoon salt
½ teaspoon pepper

½ cup green onions, tops included, chopped
1¼ cups shredded mild cheddar cheese
1 (8-ounce) carton sour cream

cheddar cheese
parsley leaves

1. Preheat oven to 400 degrees. Wash and scrub potatoes; prick with fork all over. Place potatoes on rack in oven uncovered, and bake for 45 minutes to 1 hour. Remove and let cool. Fry bacon in heavy skillet until crisp. Drain on paper towel and crumble. Set aside.

2. In large heavy saucepan, melt butter over low heat. Add flour and stir until smooth and bubbly, about 1 minute. Slowly add the milk, about 1 cup at a time, stirring constantly. Add the chicken broth, salt and pepper, and continue to stir until smooth, thick, and bubbly.

3. Cut the cooled potatoes into half-inch cubes, leaving skin on, and add to milk mixture. Add the onions, cheese, and crumbled bacon. Cook until heated through. Stir in sour cream, adding additional milk if mixture is too thick. Ladle into bowls and top with cheddar cheese and a few parsley leaves for garnish. Makes 8 to 10 cups.

(Time: 20 Minutes)

Broccoli Cheese Soup

Note: *This soup is great any time of the year, and when served with a house salad and a croissant sandwich, it will entertain family or friends. It has the look of satin, and the taste is smooth and creamy. It is especially good served with* **Crunchy Chicken Salad** *recipe found on page 69. This soup thickens as it sets.*

1 bunch broccoli florets, broken into small pieces (about 4 cups)

½ cup shredded carrots

1 ¾ cups Kitchen Basics low-sodium chicken broth

1 teaspoon chicken base or 1 chicken bouillon cube

¼ cup butter

¼ cup flour

4 cups half-and-half

10 ounces Velveeta cheese (not light), cut into small chunks

salt and pepper

1. Place broccoli, carrots, chicken broth, and chicken base in an 8-quart heavy pot. Cook together over medium heat until boiling, and then simmer 2 to 3 minutes. Remove from heat.

2. In large skillet, melt butter until bubbly. Add flour all at once and begin stirring with flat slotted spatula until smooth. Slowly add the half-and-half, stirring constantly for a smooth consistency. Add the Velveeta and continue to stir until smooth and cheese is melted into the cream.

3. Add the cheese sauce to the broccoli mixture and simmer over low heat about 8 minutes, stirring often; be careful not to burn bottom. Add salt and pepper to taste. The soup will continue to thicken as it cools. Serve with sourdough bread rolls for dipping. Serves 4.

reamy Potato Soup

Note: *This soup is a favorite on a cold night and comforts the heart and soul of the recipient. It is an old-fashioned simple recipe that is creamy and delicious. A must-have recipe to add to your soup collection.*

8 medium or 3 large baking potatoes, peeled and cut into small cubes

2 medium yellow onions, chopped small

1 teaspoon salt

water to cover potatoes, about 5 cups

4 to 6 tablespoons butter

salt and pepper to taste

1 tablespoon snipped fresh parsley, optional

½ to 1 cup half-and-half, plus more if desired

parsley sprigs

1. Place the potatoes, onions, and salt in a large 8-quart heavy pot. Add the water and cook about 25 to 30 minutes, or until very tender.

2. Mash potatoes with a potato masher, leaving some potatoes in small chunks. Continue to soft boil potatoes for a few more minutes, letting the soup thicken and stirring often to avoid burning. Add the butter, salt, pepper, and parsley.

3. Add the half-and-half ½ cup at a time, stirring until the soup is smooth and reaches desired consistency. Taste soup and add a little more salt or pepper if desired. Ladle soup into bowls and garnish with parsley sprigs.

Serve warm with your favorite salad and crackers. Serves 6.

First Prize Ham & Bean Soup

Note: *Another great country meal, ham and beans is always a top pick for any gathering. The fresh picnic ham with bone makes the difference, and when cooked up with a savory broth of celery, potatoes and onions, you may experience a little bit of heaven. Serve with* **Sweet Southern Cornbread** *recipe found on page 107.*

2 (16-ounce) packages of Great Northern
   beans, washed and picked over
12 cups water
½ portion of a 3-pound fresh picnic ham with
   bone, fat trimmed

2 large onions, chopped into small chunks
1 large tender celery stalk, chopped into
   1-inch pieces
2 medium potatoes, unpeeled, and chopped
   into small chunks
2 teaspoons salt
½ teaspoon ground black pepper

1 small onion, finely chopped
   (optional)
salt and pepper

1. Place beans, ham with bone and water in large heavy 8-quart pot. Start with 12 cups water and add additional water later if needed. Bring liquid to rolling boil and skim off any foam. Reduce heat to medium-low and partially cover. Cook, stirring occasionally, until beans begin to tender, about 1 hour.

2. Add the onions, celery, potatoes, salt, and pepper. Cook beans another 45 minutes to 1 hour. Meat should be very tender and fall off the bone. Beans should be completely cooked soft, but not mushy.

3. Remove from heat and discard bones, skin, and fat. Chop meat into small chunks and return to pot. Add salt and pepper as desired. Ladle beans into soup bowls and garnish with 1 tablespoon finely chopped onion, if desired. Serve with cornbread. Serves 6 to 8.

Ham & Bean Soup

Rosalie Serving Country

Fresh Garden Tomato Soup

Note: *This delightful homemade fresh tomato soup is hearty, with a little chunky consistency. Wait until the garden tomatoes are ripe and juicy for the best results. Served hot or cold, it tastes great.*

½ cup chopped onion

2 cloves garlic, minced

¼ cup butter

¼ cup all-purpose flour

1 cup water

½ cup Kitchen Basics low-sodium
  chicken stock

6 medium to large plump tomatoes, peeled,
  cored, and coarsely chopped (save juice)

1 tablespoon fresh parsley, minced

¼ cup fresh basil, chopped

1 tablespoon sugar

1 teaspoon salt

½ teaspoon dried whole thyme

¼ teaspoon pepper

⅛ teaspoon red pepper flakes, optional

1 bay leaf

Wheat croûtons or wheat crackers

1. Using a large heavy pot or Dutch oven, sauté onion and garlic in butter for about 2 to 3 minutes, or until tender. Reduce heat to low and add flour, stirring until smooth. Gradually add the water and chicken stock and continue to stir mixture until thick and bubbly.

2. Add the chopped tomatoes, juice included, and stir into the flour mixture. Add the parsley, basil, sugar, salt, thyme, pepper, red pepper, and bay leaf. Stir well.

3. Cover and reduce heat to low; simmer 30 minutes, stirring occasionally. Remove and discard bay leaf. Spoon ⅓ of the soup into a food processor or blender; pulse on medium to make a smooth mixture. Place processed soup in another pot and continue to process remainder of soup. Keep soup warm on low heat. Ladle hot soup into bowls garnished with wheat croûtons, or serve wheat crackers on the side. Serves 6.

Hearty Beef & Vegetable Soup

Note: *This soup is so good and full of flavor it is sure to suit the whole family. Short on time? Start it in the morning before you go to work and put it in the crock pot for all-day cooking on high. The smell of homemade soup will warm everyone's heart as they come through the door. Just ladle it up and serve with a loaf of crusty bread for dipping.*

8 cups water
2 choice beef bones, about 1½ to 2 pounds

1 pound stew meat
1 tablespoon olive oil
Lawry's coarse garlic salt with parsley added
ground black pepper

2 cups Kitchen Basics low-sodium beef broth
2 cups celery with leaves, sliced into
   1-inch slices
1 cup carrots, peeled and sliced into
   ½-inch slices
1 small onion, chopped into ½-inch pieces
1 (15-ounce) can diced tomatoes,
   juice included
1 cup unpeeled potatoes, cut into
   small chunks
4 cups cabbage, chopped

1 (8-ounce) can tomato sauce
2 cups water
2 to 3 beef bouillon cubes
salt and pepper

1. Place water and soup bones in an 8-quart heavy pot. Bring to boil and set timer for 15 minutes. Skim off foam as it rises.

2. While bones are cooking, fry stew meat in heavy skillet in olive oil. Sprinkle meat with garlic salt and pepper. Cook for about 12 to 15 minutes, until meat is browned and no longer pink. Add stew meat to bones and water. Continue to skim foam from top of broth. When foam subsides, cover and cook on medium-high for 30 minutes undisturbed.

3. Add the beef broth, celery, carrots, onion, tomatoes, potatoes, and cabbage. Bring soup back to boil and add the tomato sauce. Add 2 cups water, if needed. Add beef bouillon cubes, salt, and pepper to taste.

4. Cook soup for an additional 45 minutes, or until meat and vegetables are tender. Serve with crusty bread. Serves 6.

59

Homemade Chicken & Rice Soup

Note: *Chicken soup has long been the comfort soup prepared by mothers when their children had a cold, flu, or just a case of malaise. Brimming with fresh vegetables and rice, this soup can easily become a favorite. A wonderful soup for family, friends and guests.*

5 quarts water

1 whole soup chicken, 3 to 4 pounds

3 chicken bouillon cubes

3 stalks celery with leaves, cut in halves

2 medium carrots, peeled and halved

1 medium onion, halved

2 to 3 sprigs curly parsley

3 cups celery with leaves, cut into 1-inch slices

1 cup baby carrots, cut in halves

1 (10¾-ounce) can Campbell's Cream of Chicken Soup

½ cup whole milk

4 cups cooked Minute Rice

salt and pepper

1. Rinse chicken well in cold water and place in large heavy pot. Cover with water and bring to a rapid boil. Skim foam as it rises to the top. When foam subsides, add bouillon cubes, celery, carrots, onion, and parsley sprigs. Cover and cook over medium heat for 1 hour. Chicken will be tender and fall off the bone. Remove chicken to large platter to cool. Remove celery, carrots, and onion; discard.

2. Bring broth back to boil and add the chopped celery and baby carrots. Cover and let simmer about 15 minutes.

3. Skin chicken and remove all bones and any unsightly dark meat. Chop chicken into small pieces and return to broth. Continue cooking vegetables and chicken about 8 to 10 minutes.

4. Combine the canned chicken soup and milk and stir until smooth; add to soup. In another pot, cook rice until tender and then add to soup. Add salt and pepper as desired. Ladle into soup bowls and serve with warm bread rolls. Serves 6 to 8.

Chicken and Rice Soup

Rosalie Serving Country

Awesome Potato Salad

Note: *This was my mother, Ann Fiorino's version of potato salad. It has been handed down to her daughter and granddaughters. The sweet-sour syrup really sends this one over the top. The potatoes are smooth and so delicious, especially when served warm.*

5 pounds red potatoes

2 teaspoons salt

6 hard-boiled eggs

⅓ cup onion, chopped

⅔ cup tender celery hearts,
   with leaves, chopped

1 quart Kraft Miracle Whip or your favorite
   salad dressing

1 teaspoon yellow mustard

1 teaspoon salt

½ teaspoon fine ground black pepper

2 slices bacon

2 teaspoons red wine vinegar

1 teaspoon sugar

paprika

parsley sprigs

1. Wash and peel potatoes. Cut into 1-inch pieces. Boil potatoes in an 8-quart pot in salted water, until potatoes are tender but not mushy. Drain cooked potatoes and place in large mixing bowl. Peel eggs when cooled; chop and add to warm potatoes. Add the onion, celery, salad dressing, mustard, and salt and pepper.

2. Cook the bacon until crispy and remove from heat. Remove all but 1 tablespoon of the bacon drippings. Crunch the bacon into small pieces and return to bacon drippings. Add vinegar and sugar, then return to low heat for about 30 seconds to form thin syrup. Add all at once to the potato salad.

3. Mix together until well blended. Sprinkle top with paprika and garnish with parsley sprigs.
   Serves 12.

Five-Layer Salad with Buttermilk Dressing

Note: *This salad is an old standby that has delighted the table of many. A quick and easy salad served often in the summer at barbecues, it is welcome most any time. One serving won't be enough!*

1 large bunch Romaine lettuce
½ cup green onions, chopped
    with tops included
1 cup frozen green peas

6 strips bacon
4 hard-boiled eggs

1 packet Hidden Valley Buttermilk
    Dressing mix
1 cup mayonnaise
1 cup buttermilk

flavored croûtons, optional

1. Remove outer leaves of lettuce. Wash each leaf, drain, and pat dry. Cut leaves in fourths.

2. Arrange cut lettuce in bottom of 13 by 9-inch glass pan. Sprinkle green onions over lettuce. Next, blanch peas in hot lightly salted water for 3 minutes; drain well and sprinkle over onions.

3. Fry bacon in heavy skillet until crisp. Drain on paper towel, crumble, and scatter over layer of peas. Slice peeled, hard-boiled eggs and lay over bacon.

4. Make dressing according to packet directions, using packet mix, mayonnaise, and butter-milk. Mix in jar and shake vigorously to combine. Spread dressing completely over top of salad. Garnish with croûtons if desired. Serves 6.

Southern Salad with Strawberry Vinaigrette

Southern Salad with Strawberry Vinaigrette

Note: *This salad should be placed in a large clear salad bowl to show off the prettiness. It is not only beautiful, but very delicious. The sugar-coated pecans, fresh strawberries, and cubes of cheese are scrumptious.*

Sugar-Coated Pecans

1 cup whole pecans

2 tablespoons sugar

3 cups Romaine lettuce, chopped into 2-inch pieces

3 cups Red curly-leaf lettuce, chopped into 2-inch pieces

2 cups fresh spinach leaves, left whole

½ cup green onions, tops included, chopped small

2 cups fresh strawberries, sliced

1 cup **Sugar Coated Pecans**

1 (16-ounce) package variegated cheese cubes (such as cheddar, Swiss, and Monterey Jack).

Strawberry Vinaigrette Dressing

⅓ cup olive oil

6 tablespoons red wine vinegar

⅔ cup Smucker's Strawberry preserves

1 teaspoon coarse sea salt

¼ teaspoon ground black pepper

1. Place pecans in dry skillet with sugar. Toast pecans until they become sugar crusted, about 3 minutes. Remove to wax paper to cool.

2. Place chopped lettuce and spinach leaves in large glass bowl. Add green onions, strawberries, and **Sugar-Coated Pecans;** toss together. Scatter cheese and toss throughout salad.

2. Make **Strawberry Vinaigrette Dressing** by combining the olive oil, vinegar, strawberry preserves, salt, and pepper in a jar with lid. Shake dressing well. Pour dressing onto salad, letting it seep down through the leaves. Serve with crackers of your choice. Delicious! Serves 6 to 8.

(Time: 15 Minutes)

Wedge Salad with Blue Cheese Dressing

Note: *The Wedge Salad has become famous in the last few years and is featured at many restaurants. It looks so elegant standing upright along with the condiments and wonderful **Homemade Blue Cheese Dressing** streaming down. Make this for your special company and they will forever have a memory of goodness.*

1 large head Iceberg lettuce,
   cut into 8 wedges

1 large tomato, diced small or 2 to 3 Roma
   tomatoes, diced small

½ cup green onions with tops included,
   diced small

1 cucumber, peeled and diced small, optional

1 cup cooked crisp bacon, crumbled

1 cup **Toasted Candied Walnuts**, chopped
   (recipe found on page 226)

2 tablespoons sugar

(Time: 5 Minutes)

Homemade Blue Cheese Dressing

¼ pound crumbled blue cheese
¼ cup sour cream
⅓ cup buttermilk
1 tablespoon red wine vinegar

1 tablespoon extra virgin olive oil
1 tablespoon sugar
1 clove garlic, minced
ground black pepper

1. To make the dressing, combine the blue cheese, sour cream, buttermilk, red wine vinegar, olive oil, sugar, garlic and ground black pepper in a medium bowl. Using an electric mixer, mix all the ingredients just until combined. If possible, make the dressing earlier in the day and chill in the refrigerator for a few hours before using.

2. Inspect lettuce and remove any wilted outside leaves. On cutting board, cut the head of lettuce in half, and then into 8 wedges. Using 8 salad plates, stand each wedge on its side.

3. In large mixing bowl, combine the tomatoes, onions, cucumber, bacon, and walnuts. Mix together and evenly divide the vegetable mix over the lettuce wedges. Crumble a little blue cheese over each wedge, if desired.

4. Divide the chilled dressing over each wedge, letting it stream down over the salsa. Makes 8 wedges.

Cranberry Raspberry Salad

Note: *This is the perfect cranberry salad with just enough sweetness and tartness to make it just right. A great accompaniment for the holiday menu or any time you desire a taste for cranberries. Delicious!*

1 (12-ounce) package fresh cranberries
1½ cups granulated sugar

1 (3-ounce) package raspberry Jell-0
1 cup boiling water

1 (8-ounce) can crushed pineapple, drained
1 orange, peeled, seeded, and chopped small
1 apple, peeled, cored, and chopped small

1. Wash and drain cranberries, then grind or chop in blender or food processor. Stir the sugar into the cranberries until completely dissolved; set aside.

2. Dissolve Jell-O in boiling water and add to cranberries.

3. Add the pineapple, orange and apple to cranberry mixture and blend together. Chill the salad for several hours to gel. Serve in a pretty bowl for a lovely presentation. Serves 8 to 10.

Wilted Lettuce

Note: *I can assure that every country table has enjoyed this all-time favorite. The first tender leaf lettuce from the garden prepared with the warm sweet-sour dressing and bacon is a mouth-watering experience. If you don't have a garden, use Romaine lettuce for a great outcome. Other varieties that work are field greens, baby spinach, or endive.*

8 cups fresh garden leaf lettuce
 or 1 large bunch Romaine lettuce
4 green onions, chopped with tops included

6 slices bacon
4 tablespoons cider vinegar
4 teaspoons white sugar
½ teaspoon salt
pepper to taste

1. Wash lettuce well and place in drainer. Pat dry and tear into bite size portions; place in large bowl. Add the chopped green onions and toss together.

2. In medium heavy skillet fry bacon until crisp, drain on paper towel and crumble when cool. Leave bacon drippings in pan and add vinegar, sugar, salt, and pepper. Bring to boil, stir well, and remove from heat. Pour dressing over lettuce to "wilt." Yum! Serves 4 to 6.

Crunchy Chicken Salad

Note: *This chicken salad is so tasty you will want to make it for everyone. It is especially good for all your carry-in parties at church, school, or your place of work. Served on small or large croissants, it is a lovely display on your platter. Serve with a tall glass of **Peach Nectar Tea** recipe found on page 29, for a tea-house lunch.*

2 (12.5-ounce) cans chicken breasts, drained
½ cup celery, chopped small
2 to 3 tablespoons onion, chopped small
1 cup purple seedless grapes, whole
1 cup pecans, left whole

1 cup mayonnaise
¼ cup sour cream
1 tablespoon lemon juice
1 teaspoon sugar

red curly lettuce leaves
12 large croissants or 15 small

clusters of purple grapes
powdered sugar

1. In large bowl combine chicken, celery, onion, grapes, and pecans. Stir well to combine.

2. Make dressing by combining mayonnaise, sour cream, lemon juice, and sugar. Add to chicken mixture. Open each croissant and place 1 lettuce leaf with curly edge protruding. Place about ⅓ cup chicken salad on each leaf. Close croissant and arrange on platter. Place grape clusters in and around croissants. Dust tops of croissants with powdered sugar. Makes about 1 dozen.

69

(Time: 20 Minutes)

Summertime Melon Salad

Note: *This refreshing fruit salad is easy to make and fun to serve for your club guests or special small group. Serve it in a decorative cantaloupe to make a beautiful presentation.*

½ (12-ounce) can frozen lemonade concentrate, thawed and undiluted

½ (12-ounce) can frozen orange juice concentrate, thawed and undiluted

2 cups assorted melon balls (cantaloupe, honeydew, and watermelon)

1 cup fresh strawberries, whole

1 (20-ounce) can chunk pineapple, drained

3 small cantaloupes, halved and seeded

Mint leaves for garnish

1. Combine lemonade, and orange juice; stir well.

2. Wash and remove stems from strawberries. Combine melon balls, strawberries and pineapple in a large bowl. Pour the lemonade mixture over the fruit. Cover and chill in refrigerator for at least 2 hours.

3. Cut a decorative edge around each cantaloupe half to resemble a zig-zag or U-shape. Remove excess cantaloupe from each half to make a cavity for the fruit. Spoon fruit mixture into cantaloupe halves and garnish with mint leaves. Serve on colorful fruit plates. Serves 6.

Waldorf Salad

Note: *This salad was created by Chef Oscar Tschirky of the Waldorf-Astoria Hotel in New York in the late 1890s. In the early years of the 19th century it was considered the height of sophistication to serve it. Listed in many southern cookbooks, I wanted to include it in my list of favorite salads.*

2 tablespoons lemon juice
2 large tart red apples, cored,
  unpeeled and diced
1 large green apple, cored,
  unpeeled and diced

½ pound seedless red grapes
½ cup celery, finely diced
½ cup raisins
½ cup walnuts or pecans, left whole

½ cup mayonnaise
1 tablespoon sour cream
½ teaspoon lemon juice
1 teaspoon sugar

curly red or green leaf lettuce

1. Sprinkle lemon juice over apples in bowl; let set for 1 to 2 minutes, then drain. Combine apples with grapes, celery, raisins, and nuts.

2. Make dressing by combining mayonnaise, sour cream, lemon juice and sugar. Stir into apple mixture and serve on a large leaf of red or green leaf lettuce. Serves 6 to 8.

Vegetables, Side Dishes, and Sauces

VEGETABLES, SIDE DISHES and SAUCES

If you love vegetables, you will love this section that is filled with the best of country vegetable recipes and side dishes. Even the sauces are great such as the **Creamy Cheese Sauce** served over steamed vegetables. There are some vegetables and side dishes that only the "country folks" know how to fix.

After gathering the fruit of their gardens, you can see them sitting on their porches snapping green beans, shucking corn, or hulling peas. Canning jars are lined up on the kitchen table, ready to capture the summer's goodness.

As a young married woman, I can remember being invited to the country dinner table after moving to rural Troy, Missouri. My husband, Bill, and our three children loved the main courses, which were usually fried chicken, fried fish, or something wonderfully baked. But we eagerly looked forward to the vegetables and side dishes that were also served. There were dishes of **Broccoli Cheese Casserole** and **Candied Sweet Potatoes;** platters of **Fried Okra, Deviled Eggs,** and **Fried Apples with Cinnamon Sauce,** all laid out on a colorful linen tablecloth. The **Fresh Frozen Corn** was so sweet and buttery, it was almost like eating candy.

The hospitality was gracious, and the hosts always made sure their guests had plenty to eat. I remember on one occasion being served all vegetables and cornbread. There was no baked roast or ham; it was a celebration of the first garden vegetables. There was a large pot of **Country Green Beans with Ham,** a big bowl of **Creamy Homemade Mashed Potatoes, Asparagus in Garlic Butter Sauce, Mustard Greens Supreme,** and my children's favorite, **Creamy Macaroni & Cheese.**

The end of summer also brought great surprises, one of which was the **Fried Green Tomatoes,** which could easily become addictive. We are a blessed nation in that we have fresh fruit and vegetable markets all around us, even as close as our neighborhood grocery. Cook up one of these great dishes tonight and enjoy!

Sweet & Salty Sweet Potatoes

Note: *This recipe comes from my niece Tina Whited of Naples, Florida. It is a great way to serve sweet potatoes not only fast and easy, but so delicious. This recipe can be cut in half for 8 quarters, or left as is for sixteen. These potatoes go nicely with* **Grilled Steaks with Thyme and Lemon** *recipe found on page 150.*

4 large sweet potatoes

1 cup butter, divided
2 tablespoons coarse sea salt, divided

2 cups brown sugar, divided
cinnamon
nutmeg
crushed cloves

additional butter pats, optional

1. Preheat oven to 400 degrees. Wash and scrub potatoes, pierce with fork on all sides. Microwave potatoes for 6 minutes on one side, then turn over and microwave for 4 minutes. Remove from microwave.

2. Place potatoes on rack in oven and bake for 6 to 8 minutes, until potatoes are soft. Remove to stove top. Cut each potato in half, then in half again, making 16 quarters.

3. Melt butter and pour ½ cup in bottom of each of 2 large pie pans. Add 1 tablespoon salt to each and mix with butter. In each pan, roll 8 quarters of sweet potato until covered in butter mixture. Turn top-side up and score the tops of each sweet potato with a sharp knife back and forth to allow seasonings to seep down.

4. Sprinkle 1 cup brown sugar evenly over each of the 8 quarters in first pan. Repeat with the second pan. Sprinkle each quarter with cinnamon, nutmeg, and cloves.

5. Place the pie pans under broiler for 1 minute to caramelize the tops of each potato, being careful not to burn. Serve warm from pie pans or transfer to a ceramic round platter for a pretty presentation. Add butter pats over each quarter if desired. Serves 8 to 16.

Candied Sweet Potatoes

Note: *This dish is pure bliss! Good anytime, but especially around the Thanksgiving holiday. Even if your family doesn't like sweet potatoes, they will likely love this favorite.*

5 to 6 pounds sweet potatoes, about 5 large
8 quarts water
2 teaspoons salt

1 stick butter
2½ cups light brown sugar
1 cup pecans, left whole
cinnamon
¼ cup apple juice or water

2 cups large marshmallows

1. Preheat oven to 350 degrees. Boil sweet potatoes in salted water for about 25 to 30 minutes or until tender. Drain potatoes and let cool.

2. Peel potatoes and cut into ½-inch rounds; place in 13 by 9-inch baking dish. Cut butter into 2-inch slices and place over potatoes. Add brown sugar over butter and sprinkle with cinnamon. Add water or apple juice.

3. Bake uncovered for about 45 minutes, or until syrup becomes caramelized.

4. Remove from oven and place marshmallows over top. Return to oven and toast marshmallows to golden color, about 5 to 6 minutes. Watch carefully or they will become too dark and melt into sauce. Serve warm for best taste. Serves 8.

Sweet Potato Casserole

Note: *This is a must-have casserole over the Thanksgiving and Christmas holidays. Fresh sweet potatoes are my favorite, but if you are short on time, use canned. Your family will love the candied topping as well as the creamy sweet potatoes inside. If you are having a big crowd, just double the recipe. Delicious!*

3 large sweet potatoes cut into quarters or
   1 large can sweet potatoes in light syrup,
   about 3 cups
1 teaspoon salt

½ cup sugar
½ cup butter
½ teaspoon salt
½ teaspoon cinnamon
1 teaspoon vanilla
2 eggs, beaten
⅓ cup milk

2 cups miniature marshmallows

Crumb Topping

1 cup flour
1 stick butter
1 cup brown sugar

1 cup pecans, coarsely chopped

cinnamon

1. Preheat oven to 350 degrees. Place 3 large sweet potatoes in a heavy 3-quart pot with enough water to cover potatoes and add salt. Bring to boil and cook about 40 minutes or until sweet potatoes are tender. Remove to drainer and run cool water over potatoes. Remove skin and transfer potatoes to a large bowl; mash with a potato masher.

2. Add the sugar, butter, salt, cinnamon, vanilla, eggs, and milk. Mix by hand until smooth and creamy. Put mixture into a buttered 12 by 8-inch casserole dish. Scatter marshmallows over top of sweet potatoes; set aside.

3. Make topping by combining flour, butter, and sugar in a medium bowl. Using a pastry blender, cut the butter into the flour and sugar until mixture resembles peas. Add the pecans. Sprinkle the topping over marshmallows and sprinkle lightly with cinnamon.

4. Bake in oven for 25 minutes. Remove and place on rack. Crumb topping should look toasted and marshmallows should be puffy and golden brown. Serve warm. Serves 6.

est Instant Mashed Potatoes

Note: *While there's nothing like real mashed potatoes, there are occasions where time does not permit this luxury. These potatoes are so creamy and good, you may not be able to tell the difference. They are truly delicious! To create your own flavor, try fresh crumbled bacon, chopped green onions, or an array of cheeses.*

1½ cups water
½ whole milk
2 tablespoons butter

1¼ cups Idahoan Real Premium
   Mashed Potatoes
¼ cup cream cheese
¼ cup sour cream
1 tablespoon fresh chopped chives (optional)
salt and pepper

1. In a 3-quart heavy pot, combine water, milk, and butter. Bring liquid to boil.

2. Add the instant potatoes, cream cheese, and sour cream; stir together until mixture thickens. Add the chives, salt, and pepper to taste. If mixture is to too thick, add a little warm milk. Serves 4.

(Time: 30 Minutes)

reamy Homemade Mashed Potatoes

Note: *While this recipe is very basic and simple, you may find in this case that less is more. There are no unusual ingredients in this dish, just the basics of rich cream and real butter do the trick. Serve with* **Rosalie's Chicken & Dumplings** *recipe found on page 117, and ladle the gravy from the chicken and dumplings over the mashed potatoes. Yum!*

5 medium red potatoes (about 2½ pounds)
3 quarts water
2 teaspoons salt

¾ cup whole milk
½ cup heavy whipping cream
6 tablespoons butter
salt and pepper

1. Boil potatoes in a 3-quart heavy pot in salted water for 20 minutes, or until tender. Drain well and keep in strainer.

2. In same pot, combine milk and cream; heat until hot. Remove from heat. Place potatoes in ricer and mash through into cream mixture, or use a hand-held potato masher. Do not use an electric mixer. Stir potatoes into cream mixture and return to low heat. Continue to stir with slotted spoon; add butter, and salt and pepper to taste. Add additional milk or butter for your desired taste. Serve with or without gravy. If serving without gravy, add 1 pat butter over each serving. Serves 6 to 8.

Potatoes, with Sour Cream & Green Onions

Potatoes with Sour Cream & Green Onions

Note: *New little red potatoes are one of the joys of early summer, and when combined with a little butter and herbs like parsley, chives, or green onions, they are always a hit. Gently smash the potatoes with back of spoon, so more of the potato is covered with butter. Delicious!*

2 pounds small red new potatoes, unpeeled

2 teaspoons salt

8 tablespoons butter

¼ cup sour cream

3 to 4 green onions, finely chopped, tops included

½ teaspoon coarse sea salt

¼ teaspoon coarse ground black pepper

1. Scrub and rinse potatoes and place in a large 8-quart pot. Cover with water by about 1 inch. Add the salt and bring to boil. Cook potatoes until tender, about 15 to 20 minutes. Drain most of water, leaving about 1 tablespoon in bottom of pan.

2. Return pot to stove over very low heat. Add the butter and stir until butter melts. Keeping pan over heat, gently smash most of the potatoes into the butter and continue to heat through, about 1 to 2 minutes. Fold in sour cream until spread throughout. Fold in the onions, sea salt, and pepper. Potatoes should appear somewhat lumpy. Add more seasoning if desired. Serve warm. Makes about 6 servings.

(Time: 20 Minutes)

Fresh Frozen Corn

Note: *There is just nothing like fresh frozen corn off the cob. This dish comes straight from the garden and will complement any main dish.*

4 quarts fresh cut corn

1 quart water

1 cup sugar

4 teaspoons salt

2 tablespoons butter

1. In large heavy pot, place the corn, water, sugar, and salt. Bring to a boil and cook for 10 minutes. Cool corn and freeze, including liquid, in pint or quart zip-lock freezer bags.

2. Remove from freezer as needed and warm in small saucepan. Add butter and season to taste. Makes 5 quarts.

(Time: 35 Minutes)

Fried Okra

Note: *Fried okra is a given for the country table, especially when served with **Country Fried Catfish** recipe found on page 135. Covered with fine yellow cornmeal and deep-fried, they are light, crunchy and melt in your mouth!*

1 pound okra, fresh or frozen

1 egg, beaten

1 cup buttermilk

2 cups Martha White Self-Rising Corn Meal Mix

1 teaspoon salt

¼ teaspoon pepper

corn or canola oil

salt

1. Cut off and discard tip and stem ends from okra; cut okra into ½-inch slices. If using frozen okra, use as is. Whisk together egg and buttermilk. Pour mixture over okra in bowl and let set for 15 to 30 minutes.

2. In large bowl, combine the cornmeal, salt, and pepper. With slotted spoon, remove a spoonful of okra and let buttermilk mixture drain through slots. Place okra in the cornmeal and turn until well coated. Place on cookie sheet until ready to fry. Continue to dredge okra in cornmeal.

3. Pour oil to depth of 2 inches in a 10-inch cast iron skillet or Dutch oven and heat to 350 degrees. Fry okra in batches about 3 to 4 minutes, until golden brown. Sprinkle lightly with salt while frying. Remove to paper towels to drain. Arrange on pretty platter and serve. Serves 4 to 6.

Fried Green Tomatoes

Note: *Fried green gomatoes are wonderful coated with flour or cornmeal and fried in oil. Pick them green or greenish orange while nice and firm. They pair nicely with chicken or fish, or do as some country folk and let it be the main entrée. I used a mild olive oil for a wonderful taste. A large tomato will yield about 8 slices. You will love these!*

⅓ cup olive oil, plus more if needed

2 to 3 large tomatoes
1 egg beaten
1 cup buttermilk

2 cups self-rising yellow or white corn meal, fine grind
1 teaspoon salt
¼ teaspoon ground black pepper

salt and pepper
parsley sprigs

1. Place the olive oil in a large deep skillet and turn the heat to medium-high right before dredging tomatoes.

2. Core the tomatoes, and dip into boiling water for 30 seconds to peel the skin, if desired. Or consider leaving peelings intact. Cut the tomatoes crosswise into ¼-inch slices. Whisk together the egg and buttermilk, and place in shallow dish.

3. In large bowl, combine the cornmeal, salt and pepper. Dip tomato slices in buttermilk mixture, then dredge the tomatoes on both sides in the cornmeal mixture. Place the tomatoes in the hot oil to sizzle, watching not to burn. Turn when the first side is golden brown, then fry the other side, about 6 to 8 minutes total. Sprinkle the slices lightly with salt and pepper as they fry. Remove to paper towels to drain, and place on pretty platter garnished with parsley sprigs. Serves 4 to 6.

(Time: 25 Minutes)

Country Green Beans with Ham or Bacon

Note: *These tender green beans don't have to cook all day for good flavor. They are best seasoned with thick sliced bacon or left-over ham steak. This is an ever-popular country side dish to accompany most any meal. Try it with **Rosalie's Chicken & Dumplings** recipe found on page 117 or with **Favorite Meat Loaf** recipe found on page 128.*

left-over ham steak or 3 slices thick bacon,
   chopped

1 pound fresh green beans,
   ends cut and left whole
salt and coarse ground black pepper
¼ cup water

1. In large skillet, fry bacon until crisp. If using ham steak, add 1 to 2 tablespoons bacon drippings and fry until browned. Add the green beans and salt and pepper. Add water and cover. Cook, stirring occasionally, about 15 minutes or until green beans are crisp tender. Serves 4.

Buttermilk Battered Onion Rings

Note: *These crunchy battered onion rings are so good, they will be eaten before you get them on the table. Using a mixture of flour, cornmeal, and buttermilk, the batter is the best part. One giant Vidalia onion makes about 25 rings, which is a nice platter, but for a family of five or more hungry ones, you may want to double the recipe.*

1 large sweet Vidalia onion (about 1 pound)

1 cup buttermilk
1 large egg

1 cup all-purpose flour
⅓ cup stone ground cornmeal, medium grind
2 teaspoons coarse ground sea salt
½ teaspoon ground black pepper
½ teaspoon paprika
2 teaspoons Tone's Louisiana Style
   Cajun seasoning

2 cups corn or vegetable oil
salt

1. Preheat oven to 225 degrees. Peel onion and cut tips from each end. Slice onion with long serrated knife into ½ to ¾ -inch thick slices.

2. In medium bowl, beat together the buttermilk and egg. Separate onion rings and let soak in the buttermilk mixture for at least 15 minutes.

3. In baking dish, combine the flour, cornmeal, salt, pepper, paprika, and Cajun seasoning. Toss together until blended; set aside.

4. Using a large heavy skillet or Dutch oven heat oil to medium-high, about 350 degrees. The oil is ready when a sprinkle of flour dropped into the oil pops. Using a fork or tongs, drop onion rings into buttermilk mixture and then dredge lightly in flour/cornmeal coating. Dip again into buttermilk and back into flour/cornmeal to get a thick coating. Drop by batches into hot oil, about 4 to 5 at a time; do not crowd. Fry about 2 minutes, turning once or twice, until golden brown. Lightly salt rings while they are frying. Remove onion rings to a paper towel-lined baking pan to drain. To keep onion rings warm and crisp, place pan in warm oven while frying the next batch.

5. Remove from oven and serve from warm baking pan. Serves 4.

Hush Puppy Patties

Hush Puppy Patties

Note: *This is a recipe I happened on when using the remainder of the breading from my fried okra. I just added the buttermilk mixture to the leftover breading along with some chopped green onions and fried them up. They were more like a patty, crispy on the outside, moist on the inside, and delicious! For rave reviews, serve them with the **Country Fried Catfish** recipe found on page 135.*

1 cup corn or mild olive oil

1 cup buttermilk

1 egg, beaten

⅓ cup green onion, chopped
   with tops included

1 tablespoon fresh chives, finely chopped
   or 1 teaspoon dried chives

¼ teaspoon crushed red pepper flakes

1 ½ cups Martha White Self Rising
   Cornmeal Mix

½ teaspoon salt

¼ teaspoon ground black pepper

1. Preheat oven to 200 degrees. In large heavy skillet, pour about 2 inches of oil, set aside.

2. In large bowl, whisk together the buttermilk and beaten egg. Stir in the onion, chives, and red pepper flakes.

3. Add the cornmeal, salt, and pepper and stir into the buttermilk mixture. Let the batter rise for 1 to 2 minutes.

4. Heat the oil over medium-high heat about 350 degrees. Drop 1 tablespoon of batter at a time into the hot oil; do not crowd. Fry the hush puppies about 1 minute on each side until golden brown and crispy, lowering the heat so as not to burn. Drain on paper towels and keep warm in the oven until ready to serve. Makes about 2 dozen.

(Time: 15 Minutes)

Steamed Sweet Carrots

Note: *Carrots are wonderful when steamed with butter and a teaspoon or two of sugar. This recipe is just a simple version of an ever-faithful standby.*

1 pound baby carrots, cleaned
   and ends trimmed
1 teaspoon salt

¼ cup butter
1 tablespoon sugar
½ teaspoon salt

1. Place carrots in 3-quart heavy pot and add water just to cover top of carrots. Add salt and bring to boil. Reduce heat to medium and simmer carrots to just tender, about 10 minutes. Drain and set aside.

2. Melt butter in saucepan and add carrots. Sprinkle with sugar and salt; toss to coat well. Serves 6.

(Time: 30 Minutes)

Buttered Brussels Sprouts

Note: *Country folk love fresh vegetables, and Brussels sprouts are no exception. These are miniature cabbages, and the smaller the better is a good rule. Even if you don't think you like Brussels sprouts, I beg you to try this wonderful recipe. Serve it as a great side dish with the any pork entrée.*

1 pound small fresh Brussels sprouts
2 quarts water
1 teaspoon salt

2 tablespoon butter
1 tablespoon extra virgin olive oil
3 cloves garlic, chopped
½ teaspoon salt
ground black pepper

1. Wash and drain Brussels sprouts. Place in a 3-quart pot with water and salt. Bring to boil and cook for 20 minutes, or until tender; drain well.

2. Place the butter, olive oil and garlic in a medium skillet. Sauté the garlic for about 30 seconds, being careful not to burn. Add the Brussels sprouts, salt, and pepper and sauté for about 8 minutes, turning the sprouts often. With a spoon or fork, cut some off the sprouts in half while frying. The Brussels sprouts should be golden brown and tender. Serves 4.

Harvard Beets

Note: *I'm not sure how country this dish is, but farmers' wives have used beets for a side dish as long as beets have been around. This sweet/sour version is one of my favorites, and when fixed with small beets makes a pretty accompaniment.*

12 very small beets or 4 medium
1 teaspoon salt

⅔ cup sugar
1 tablespoon cornstarch
½ teaspoon salt
2 whole cloves
1 cup reserved beet juice
½ cup cider vinegar

2 tablespoons butter
1 tablespoon orange juice, optional

1. Leave root and one inch of stem on beets; scrub with a vegetable brush. Place beets in a heavy 3-quart pot and add water to cover. Add salt and bring to a boil. Cover and reduce heat to gentle boil; cook beets until tender, about 35 to 40 minutes. Drain beets reserving 1 cup beet juice. Pour cold water over beets and trim off stems and roots. Rub off skins and quarter beets (about 4 cups).

2. In heavy saucepan, combine sugar, cornstarch, salt, and cloves. Stir in reserved beet juice and vinegar. Cook over medium heat until thick and translucent, about 6 to 7 minutes. Add beets, butter, and orange juice, stir to combine, and heat through, about 5 minutes. Remove cloves. Serves 4 to 6.

Mustard Greens Supreme

Mustard Greens Supreme

Note: *Country folk and Southerners alike love greens, especially cooked up with bacon, ham hocks, or salt pork. Any one of the following greens can be used: mustard, kale, collards, Swiss chard, or even a combination. I used the potatoes once while trying to tone down extra salt that I accidentally put in the greens and just left them in; they were great! I added them as an optional item.*

2 pounds mustard greens,
   tough stems removed

½ pound thick sliced bacon,
   cut into 1-inch pieces

2 small onions, chopped small

2 cloves garlic, chopped small

2 cups Kitchen Basics low-sodium
   chicken broth

1 teaspoon salt

½ teaspoon crushed red pepper flakes

ground black pepper

2 tablespoons cider vinegar

1 teaspoon Worcestershire sauce

1 teaspoon sugar

2 small red potatoes, cut into small chunks,
   optional

salt and pepper

1. Wash greens several times in cool water and rinse well; drain in colander. Place on wooden chopping block and cut tough stems from leaves; cut greens crosswise in 3 to 4-inch pieces; set aside.

2. Place bacon in heavy skillet and fry until crisp. Transfer bacon and drippings to heavy pot or Dutch oven and add onion and garlic. Sauté for about 5 to 6 minutes, or until the onion is golden.

3. Add greens and toss with the bacon mixture. Add the chicken broth, salt, red pepper flakes, and pepper. Bring greens to boil and add the vinegar, Worcestershire sauce, and sugar. If using the potatoes, add them now. Cover and cook for about 20 to 30 minutes or until desired tenderness. Thicker greens may need a longer time to cook. Add any additional salt or pepper as desired. Serves 6.

(Time: 35 Minutes)

Broccoli Cheese Casserole

Note: *This is an ever-popular side dish that warms the heart and the soul. Creamy and hearty with chunks of broccoli lathered in cheese sauce, this is good for kids and adults.*

¼ cup butter

1 bunch broccoli florets

1 small onion

½ cup celery, finely chopped

1 teaspoon salt

¼ teaspoon ground black pepper

1 (10¾-ounce) can cream of chicken soup

1 cup milk

4 ounces Velveeta Cheese (not light)

½ cup Kitchen Basics low-sodium
   chicken stock

1½ cups prepared Minute Rice

salt and pepper

1. Preheat oven to 350 degrees. In large skillet, melt butter. Add broccoli florets, onion, celery, salt, and pepper. Stir fry until celery and onion are translucent and broccoli is tender, about 8 to 10 minutes.

2. Combine chicken soup and milk until well blended; stir into broccoli mixture. Add the cheese and chicken stock and stir over low heat until creamy. Add the rice; stir mixture together. Add seasoning, if desired.

3. Pour broccoli mixture into a buttered 13 by 9-inch casserole dish and bake for 15 minutes, or until casserole is set. Serves 4 to 6.

Max, Grant &
Roman Harpole

Alexandra Harpole

Creamy Macaroni & Cheese

Creamy Macaroni & Cheese

Note: *Macaroni and cheese could be one of America's favorite foods, not to mention a Southernism from way back. One could write a book on the many ways to prepare this dish. This recipe is simple, creamy, smooth, and delicious. I used the medium cheddar, but you may prefer a more sharper taste.*

4 cups elbow macaroni

2 teaspoons salt

½ cup butter

4 tablespoons all-purpose flour

4 cups whole milk

½ cup heavy cream, plus more if needed

¼ teaspoon ground black pepper

¼ teaspoon ground red pepper

½ teaspoon Lawry's coarse garlic salt
  with parsley

4 cups medium cheddar cheese, shredded
  or 1 (16-ounce) brick, cut into chunks

4 ounces Velveeta Cheese (not light)

¾ cup additional cheddar cheese, shredded

paprika

1 tablespoon butter

½ cup dried bread crumbs

1. Preheat oven to 350 degrees. Cook macaroni in an 8-quart heavy pot with 2 teaspoons salt added, about 8 minutes. Drain; set aside in a large bowl.

2. Melt butter in same 8-quart pot until sizzling; stir in flour. Cook over medium heat, stirring occasionally, until smooth and bubbly, about 1 minute. Add milk and cream slowly until mixture is smooth. Add pepper, red pepper, and garlic salt, blending well.

3. Add the 4 cups of cheese and Velveeta; stir until completely blended. Mix with the drained macaroni. Pour mixture into a 11 by 15-inch buttered dish.

4. Sprinkle the ¾ cup shredded cheese over the top of macaroni. Sprinkle paprika over the cheese. In a small saucepan, melt butter. Add the bread crumbs just to moisten and sprinkle over cheese.

5. Cover with foil and bake 15 minutes or until mixture is warmed through and bubbly. Serves 8.

(Time: 15 Minutes)

sparagus in Garlic Butter Sauce

Note: *There is nothing so sweet as fresh-cut asparagus fried to crisp-tender in a light butter sauce. This is one side dish you will love to prepare and serve with most any main course. Awesome!*

1 pound fresh young asparagus ends trimmed

2 cloves fresh garlic, finely chopped

2 tablespoons extra virgin olive oil

2 tablespoons butter

coarse sea salt

fresh coarse ground black pepper

1. Wash and rinse asparagus and trim off tough ends; cut into thirds. In large skillet, place the asparagus, olive oil and chopped garlic. Sauté the asparagus over medium heat for 8 to 10 minutes, or until crisp-tender. Salt and pepper the asparagus while frying. Add the butter during the last minute of frying and stir in well. Add additional salt or pepper as desired. Transfer to platter and serve warm. Serves 4.

Baked Beans

Note: *Baked beans are a staple that can always complement common everyday meals. A hearty dish that is filling and comforting, this simple recipe features down-home goodness!*

3 (15-ounce) cans pork and beans

1 to 2 slices thick bacon, optional

½ cup brown sugar

1 small onion, finely chopped

2 teaspoons mustard

⅓ cup ketchup

1. Preheat oven to 350 degrees. Place beans in a heavy 3-quart pot. If using bacon, fry until crisp, being careful not to burn. Crunch up bacon and add to beans.

2. Add brown sugar, onion, mustard, and ketchup; stir until blended. Bring mixture to boil on stove; cover and simmer 5 to 10 minutes. Transfer to a 2-quart casserole dish and bake in oven uncovered about 25 to 30 minutes, stirring occasionally. Makes 1½ quarts.

Deviled Eggs

Note: *Everyone loves deviled eggs in the summertime, especially with barbeque. These eggs are so simple to make, you can whip them up in 20 minutes and have them anytime.*

8 eggs

½ cup Miracle Whip, or mayonnaise

1 teaspoon mustard

1 teaspoon red wine vinegar

1 tablespoon pickle relish

salt and pepper

paprika

parsley sprig

1. Place room-temperature eggs in pot of cold water. Eggs should be covered by about 2 inches of water. Bring to boil and cook eggs about 15 minutes. Remove from heat; drain and keep under cool water.

2. Peel egg shells and rinse. Cut eggs in half lengthwise and remove the yolks to a medium bowl. Wipe knife between each cut to make a clean sliced egg. Place white halves on pretty egg tray or platter.

3. Mash the yolks with fork slightly and add the mayonnaise and mustard. Using a whisk, smooth out the yolk mixture until all lumps are gone. Fold in the vinegar and pickle relish, and add salt, and pepper to taste. Mix with spoon until smooth.

4. Refill the whites using about a tablespoon of the yolk mixture for each egg half. Garnish each egg with a sprinkle of paprika. Place parsley sprig in center of platter. Makes 16 eggs.

Fried Apples with Cinnamon Sauce

Note: *Want a taste of apple pie? These fried apples could easily go into pie crust, but instead they are the perfect side dish with your favorite country meal. They go especially good with any pork or meat entrée.*

5 to 6 Granny Smith apples, peeled, cored and
   sliced, about 4 cups
¼ cup butter
2 teaspoons lemon juice
2 teaspoons flour

½ cup brown sugar
½ cup white sugar
½ teaspoon apple pie spice
¼ teaspoon cinnamon

2 to 3 teaspoons heavy cream

1. In large skillet, melt butter and fry apples over medium heat about 6 to 8 minutes, or until the apples are tender. Sprinkle apples with lemon juice. Sprinkle flour over apples and continue to stir until apples are coated.

2. Add brown sugar, white sugar, apple pie spice and cinnamon. Continue to stir until apples are coated and golden brown. Stir cream into mixture to make a thick sauce. Remove from heat and serve. Serves 6.

Buttermilk Coleslaw

Note: *This creamy coleslaw is a mouthful of delight. Always a favorite, it is especially good with the **Southern Fried Chicken** recipe found on page 121, or any one of the many country suppers in this book. For a light bite, use Splenda instead of sugar, it works great.*

2 (10-ounce) packages shredded cabbage mix	3 tablespoons lemon juice
⅓ cup carrot, shredded	1 tablespoon cider vinegar
½ cup sugar or 3 teaspoons Splenda	salt and pepper
½ cup Miracle Whip or mayonnaise	
½ cup buttermilk	

1. In large bowl, combine cabbage and carrot. Whisk together sugar, mayonnaise, buttermilk, lemon juice, and cider vinegar. Pour over cabbage and toss together well. Salt and pepper coleslaw as desired. Cover and chill in refrigerator until ready to serve. Serves 8.

Sweet & Sour Coleslaw

Note: *This coleslaw is a little different than the usual creamy style and has a tangy sweet-sour taste. It's almost addictive once you taste it, and it even gets better kept in the refrigerator. I made it with Splenda for my husband and he liked it better than with the white sugar. Everyone will want this recipe. Serve with **Country Fried Catfish** recipe found on page 135.*

1 (16-ounce) package shredded cabbage mix	½ cup mild olive oil
¾ cup shredded carrots	1 teaspoon yellow mustard,
¾ cup celery, small diced, optional	or 1 teaspoon dry mustard
1 medium red onion, chopped small	½ to 1 teaspoon salt
	¼ teaspoon black pepper
½ cup white sugar	
or 2 to 3 teaspoons Splenda	large red or green lettuce leaves
½ cup cider vinegar	

1. In large bowl, place cabbage, carrots, celery, and onion. Toss together; set aside.

2. In medium bowl combine sugar or Splenda, vinegar, olive oil, mustard, salt, and pepper. Microwave on high for about 1 to 2 minutes, or until mixture is warm and sugar is dissolved. Pour over slaw mixture and toss until completely coated. Serve over decorative lettuce leaves for a pretty presentation. Serves 8 to 10.

Country Chicken Gravy

Note: *Fried chicken just wouldn't be complete without creamy chicken gravy. This is white gravy made with chicken broth for extra flavor. Use the drippings from frying the chicken, and include any bits of chicken coating left behind.*

Pan drippings from fried chicken, about ¼ cup

¼ cup all-purpose flour

1 cup Kitchen Basics low sodium chicken broth

2 cups whole milk

½ teaspoon salt

¼ teaspoon ground black pepper

1. Using same skillet in which chicken was fried, pour off all drippings except ¼ cup, keeping any bits of chicken coating. Turn heat to medium and add the flour all at once. Stir until flour bubbles and begins to turn golden brown. Gradually add the chicken broth and milk, stirring constantly, until gravy becomes thick and bubbly. Stir in salt and pepper. Serve hot. Makes 3 cups gravy.

Creamy Cheese Sauce

Note: *This sauce can be used over vegetables such as broccoli, cauliflower, potatoes, or in casseroles. It can also be used as a basis for cream soups. A wonderful sauce that is smooth and creamy and ever so versatile, you will use this recipe often.*

¼ cup butter
¼ cup flour
1 cup Kitchen Basics low-sodium chicken broth
1 teaspoon chicken base, or 1 chicken bouillon cube

3 cups half-and-half
8 ounces Velveeta cheese (not light) cut into small chunks
   or 8 ounces mild or sharp cheddar cheese
salt and pepper

1. In large skillet over medium-low heat, melt butter until bubbly. Add flour all at once and begin stirring with flat slotted spatula until smooth. Slowly add the chicken broth and chicken base. Stir constantly for a smooth consistency.

2. When sauce begins to thicken, add the half-and-half, 1 cup at a time, stirring often. Add the Velveeta or cheddar cheese and continue to stir until smooth and cheese is melted into the cream. Cook 1 minute longer, stirring constantly so as not to burn. If sauce is too thick, add a little more cream. Add salt and pepper as desired. Makes about 4½ cups sauce.

(Time: 10 Minutes)

Mushroom Beef Gravy

Note: *This gravy will definitely compliment your steaks, hamburgers, or chops. Even without beef drippings, the result is awesome! If you do have drippings from your fried or roasted meat, by all means use them instead of the butter. Either way this recipe will work fine.*

3 tablespoons butter, or 3 to 4 tablespoons
   meat drippings
½ cup chopped onions
1 cup thin, sliced mushrooms
1 cup Kitchen Basics low-sodium beef broth
1 to 2 beef bouillon cubes

2 tablespoons flour
⅓ cup cool water
salt and pepper

1. In medium skillet, melt butter or use meat drippings. Add onions and over medium heat, sauté for 2 minutes. Add mushrooms and continue to cook for 1 to 2 minutes longer, or until onions and mushrooms are browned. Add the beef broth and bouillon cubes. Bring liquid to gentle boil.

2. Dissolve the flour into the water to make a smooth consistency. Slowly pour the flour mixture into the beef broth, stirring until desired consistency is reached. Add salt and pepper as desired. Makes about 2½ cups.

(Time: 10 Minutes)

Beef Gravy with Celery & Onions

Note: *No roast in the oven, but still want some gravy? This is a great gravy that can be served with your **Best Instant Mashed Potatoes** recipe found on page 77. Along with your meat and salad, you can serve supper in 30 minutes.*

3 tablespoons butter
⅓ cup chopped celery
⅓ cup chopped onion
2 cups Kitchen Basics low sodium beef broth

2 tablespoons flour
⅓ cup cool water
salt and pepper

1. In large skillet over medium-low heat, melt butter. Sauté the celery and onion together in butter about 2 to 3 minutes. Celery and onion will look translucent and become tender. Add the beef broth; bring liquid to gentle boil.

2. Dissolve the flour into the water to make a smooth consistency. Slowly pour the flour mixture into the beef broth, stirring until desired consistency is reached. Add salt and pepper as desired. Makes about 2½ cups.

Tartar Sauce

Note: *There is nothing like homemade sauces and this recipe is no exception. Used over baked or fried fish, this adds just the touch.*

1 cup mayonnaise

3 tablespoons sweet pickle relish

1 tablespoon capers, optional

1 teaspoon lemon juice

dash of hot sauce

1 teaspoon spicy mustard

minced fresh parsley

1. Combine the mayonnaise, sweet pickle relish, capers, lemon juice, hot sauce, and mustard. Mix together well; cover and chill before serving. Garnish with the minced parsley. Makes 1¼ cups.

(Time: 10 Minutes)

Zesty Cocktail Sauce

Note: *It is fun to make your own homemade sauces, and much less expensive too. This sauce has a zing and is great for cocktail or fried shrimp. Make it up and store it in the refrigerator, will keep up to 1 month.*

⅔ cup chili sauce

1 tablespoon lemon juice

2 to 3 tablespoons prepared horseradish

2 teaspoons Worcestershire sauce

¼ teaspoon hot sauce.

1. Combine the chili sauce, lemon juice, horseradish, Worcestershire sauce, and hot sauce. Blend together until smooth. Cover and chill at least 2 hours before serving. Makes 1 cup.

BREADS and ROLLS

SMELL THAT BREAD

While teaching cooking classes, I usually try to include **Rosalie's Homemade Bread** recipe. Not only is the outcome rewarding, especially with the crust being crunchy and the inside dense and meaty, but the smell of the cooking bread is heavenly! Its aroma fills the kitchen with anticipated joy, and there is just nothing like it.

Many think they are too busy to bake bread, but it can be started it in the morning before going to work. One of my students told how she put the bread together before she left for work. She put it in the refrigerator and gave the bread plenty of room to rise. When she came home, she took it out and let it come to room temperature. She then made it into loaves, and let it rise again. While it was rising, she picked the children up from their after-school activities and even ran a few errands. By the time her husband came home from work, the bread was in the oven and the scent of the baking bread sent him back out--only to pick up some flowers of appreciation for his wife baking the homemade bread. Just the smell of that bread can bring so much joy and unity.

The recipes in this section are wonderful, and it would definitely be hard to choose which one to try first. For the church supper or ladies club, the **Poppy Seed Bread with Orange Glaze** will always make a hit. The rich delightful almond and orange flavor together with the crunch of poppy seeds is almost indescribable.

For the country meal of **Chicken & Dumplings,** the **Sweet Yeast Rolls** are a must, and very easy to make. They will literally melt in your mouth. For a luncheon with friends, no one will ever turn away the ever-popular **Sally Lunn Bread.** And when making a big pot of H**am & Beans,** the **Sweet Southern Cornbread** slathered with butter will send this dish over the top.

Lastly, **Rosalie's Dinner Rolls** will gladly complement any hearty soup, especially right out of the oven and eaten warm. They are also great dipped into the broth.

So, my friend, be sure to bake the heavenly bread, rolls, and cornbread. Your family will love you for it and it may even start a tradition for your children and grandchildren to follow. You'll be hooked the first time you "Smell that Bread!"

Rosalie's Cheddar Cheese Biscuits

Note: *These biscuits are so great, they actually melt in your mouth. Topped with warm garlic butter, one biscuit will not be enough!*

2 cups Bisquick baking mix
⅔ cup buttermilk
¾ cup sharp shredded cheddar cheese

¼ cup butter
½ teaspoon garlic powder

1. Preheat oven to 450 degrees. Combine baking mix, milk, and cheese with a wooden spoon until soft dough forms.

2. Beat vigorously 15 to 30 seconds.

3. Drop dough by heaping tablespoons onto an ungreased cookie sheet about 1 inch apart. Bake 8 to 10 minutes until golden brown.

4. Combine butter and garlic powder; brush over warm biscuits before removing from cookie sheet. Serve warm. Makes 10 large biscuits.

Poppy Seed Bread with Orange Glaze

Poppy Seed Bread with Orange Glaze

Note: *This wonderful bread is especially good served warm and is great for breakfast or any meal. The almond orange glaze is amazing, and coupled with the buttery bread, this is a keeper recipe. I used mild olive oil instead of vegetable oil for a great taste and moistness.*

3 cups all-purpose flour

2¼ cups granulated sugar

2 tablespoons poppy seeds

1½ teaspoons baking powder

1½ teaspoons salt

3 eggs

1½ cups milk

1¼ cups mild olive oil

1½ teaspoons vanilla extract

1½ teaspoons almond extract

1½ teaspoons butter extract

Glaze

¾ cup granulated sugar

¼ cup orange juice

1 teaspoon vanilla extract

1 teaspoon almond extract

1 teaspoon butter extract

1. Preheat oven to 350 degrees. In large bowl combine flour, sugar, poppy seeds, baking powder, and salt; set aside.

2. In smaller bowl, combine eggs, milk, oil, vanilla extract, almond extract and butter extract. Beat mixture until well blended and add to the dry flour mixture. Stir ingredients until blended and smooth. Butter and dust with flour 2 (9 by 5-inch) loaf pans or 6 mini loaf pans. Pour batter into prepared pans and bake for 55 to 60 minutes, or until bread springs back when touched.

3. While loaves are baking, prepare glaze. In small saucepan, combine sugar, orange juice, vanilla extract, almond extract, and butter extract. Bring mixture to a boil and remove pan from heat. As soon as loaves come out of oven, poke holes in bread with a fork and pour prepared glaze evenly over both loaves of bread. Cool for 5 to 10 minutes, then run a butter knife along edges and gently loosen sides and bottom. Remove bread to a wooden board or platter and slice while still warm. Serves 12 slices per loaf.

Sweet Southern Cornbread

Sweet Southern Cornbread

Note: *This sweet cornbread is indescribably delicious. It has a wonderful moist texture with a satin crunchy feel to your taste. It was voted the best by the nurses and doctors at the hospital where I work part-time as a nurse. The secret is the stone-ground 100% whole grain cornmeal. Be sure to ask for Bob's Red Mill Cornmeal, medium grind. The large grind is too crunchy, but the medium is just right. It is especially good with my* **First Prize Ham & Bean Soup** *recipe found on page 56. This recipe makes a large pan so everyone can come back for seconds.*

1½ cups Bob's Red Mill Cornmeal,
   medium grind
1½ cups granulated sugar
12 tablespoons real butter (no substitutions)
3 beaten eggs

2¼ cups all-purpose flour
1 tablespoon baking powder
½ teaspoon salt

1 cup half-and-half
butter

1. Preheat oven to 350 degrees. In a large bowl, combine cornmeal and sugar; set aside. Melt butter in small pan or microwave; set aside. Beat the eggs, and together with melted butter, pour over cornmeal mixture. Mix together well, but do not beat.

2. In another bowl, combine the flour, baking powder, and salt.

3. Alternately, add flour and half-and-half to cornmeal mixture, ending with flour, and mixing only until moistened. Do not over mix. Prepare a 13 by 9-inch baking pan or 1 large (6 cup) cupcake pan by coating bottom and sides with melted butter. Spoon cornmeal mixture into pan and let sit for 5 minutes.

4. Bake in prepared oven for 25 to 30 minutes, or until cornbread is set and inserted toothpick comes out dry. Remove pan from oven and serve warm with butter and honey if desired. Makes 24 servings.

Rosalie's Dinner Rolls

Rosalie's Dinner Rolls

Note: *These rolls are dense and crusty on the outside and earthy on the inside. They are great for dipping in soup or to accompany stews. You will also love the heavenly smell that will fill the kitchen. Serve warm from the oven to accompany* **Roast Beef & Noodles** *recipe found on page 130 and* **Farmer's Cabbage** *recipe found on page 125.*

1¼ cups warm water
3 teaspoons yeast

4½ cups bread flour
2 teaspoons salt
1 egg, beaten
2 tablespoons butter, melted

1 tablespoon olive oil for coating dough
1 (14-inch) pizza stone
2 tablespoons yellow cornmeal

1 egg white
1 tablespoon water
sesame seeds, optional

1. Preheat oven to 400 degrees. Put yeast in warm water and stir to dissolve, letting it foam up for 8 to 10 minutes.

2. Place the flour in a large bowl, add the salt and mix well. Make a "well" in the center of the flour; add the egg and melted butter and work into the flour, dribbling yeast water a little at a time. Work the liquid into the flour until all is incorporated. Bring all the dough together into a ball and knead 8 to 10 minutes, until dough feels elastic. If the dough is sticky, add a little more flour. Pour the olive oil over the dough and turn to coat. Let rise in a warm place for 1½ to 2 hours.

3. Punch the dough down and let it rest for 15 minutes on counter. Divide the dough into 12 pieces and shape into rolls. Dust the stone with cornmeal and place the rolls on the stone. Cover rolls with towel, and let rise another hour or until doubled in size.

4. Beat the egg white with water until foamy. Brush the rolls with the egg white mixture and sprinkle with sesame seeds, if desired. Bake in hot oven 20 minutes or until golden. Makes 12 large rolls.

Rosalie's Homemade Bread

Note: *My mother, Ann Fiorino, would make this bread often while I was growing up. Although we called it Italian Bread, it would fit wonderfully in the country setting. Warm out of the oven, this bread is definitely worth your effort. Short on time? Put it together before you go to work. Place it in the refrigerator in a large bowl covered with plastic wrap. Punch it down when you get home and make into loaves; let rise and bake. Wonderful served with **Hearty Beef Soup** recipe found on page 59.*

6½ to 7 cups bread flour, or all-purpose flour

3 teaspoons salt

2 tablespoons active dry yeast

2 cups warm water, not hot to touch, about 110 degrees

1 tablespoon olive oil

1 (14-inch) pizza stone

2 tablespoons yellow cornmeal

1 egg, beaten

1 tablespoon water

sesame seeds

1. Preheat oven to 400 degrees. Place 6½ cups flour and salt in large bowl or pan and mix together. Put yeast in warm water and stir to dissolve, letting it foam up for 8 to 10 minutes. Make a "well" in the flour mixture and add a little of the yeast water with a small amount of flour, working together and setting to side of bowl. Continue until all the flour and water have been used. Bring all the dough together; dough may be sticky. Work in the remaining ½ cup flour as needed. If dough comes together firm, you will not need the additional flour. Knead together 8 to 10 minutes until dough feels elastic. Pour olive oil over dough, turning to coat entire surface. Place towel over dough and let rise in warm place, 1½ to 2 hours, until doubled in size.

2. Punch dough down and let dough rise another 1 hour. (If pressed for time, bypass this rising and go to step 3)

3. After the second rising, sprinkle cornmeal on stone. Punch dough down and divide into three parts, shaping each part into a loaf. Place loaves 2 inches apart on stone. With a serrated knife, make 3 slits across the top of each loaf. Beat the egg and water together and brush the top of each loaf with the egg wash; sprinkle with sesame seeds. Place warm loose towel over the top of loaves, and let rise until double in size, about 1 hour.

4. Place stone on middle grate in oven and bake bread for 30 to 35 minutes. The bread will have a golden hard crust. Remove bread from oven and let cool 5 to 10 minutes before slicing. Serve warm with butter. Yields: 3 loaves.

Nicholas, Rosalie,
Alexandra & Reagan

Sweet Yeast Rolls

Sweet Yeast Rolls

Note: *These are the famous yeast rolls that were served from our Country Kitchen during the Old Thresher's Country Fair, held yearly in Elsberry, Missouri. They were made right on the spot from morning until the last meal was served. People would stand in line for a hot roll, and it was said that they walked around the Fair Grounds holding a hot roll rather than funnel cakes or cotton candy. You will always cherish this recipe.*

2 tablespoons yeast
¼ cup warm water

3 eggs, beaten
1 cup luke-warm water
½ cup melted butter

5½ cups flour, divided
2 teaspoons salt
⅔ cup sugar

½ cup melted butter, divided
½ cup sugar, divided

melted butter
sugar

1. Preheat oven to 400 degrees. Dissolve yeast in ¼ cup warm water using fork to mix thoroughly. Set timer and let stand 10 minutes. Yeast will foam up high and look pasty.

2. In large glass bowl, add beaten eggs, 1 cup lukewarm water, ½ cup melted butter and the foamy yeast; stir together.

3. Add 3 cups flour, salt, and sugar to wet ingredients; dough will be sticky. Add additional 2 cups flour and turn out onto floured surface. If dough is still too sticky, add the remainder flour and knead together gently. Do not overwork dough. Coat glass bowl with olive oil or cooking spray. With floured hands, place dough in bowl. Dough should be very soft. Cover with towel and place on top of stove in a warm place. Let rise to double in size, about 1 to 1½ hours.

4. Place dough on floured surface; cut dough ball in half. Roll dough with rolling pin, dusting lightly with flour as needed, to a 12 by 15-inch rectangle. With pastry brush, brush dough with ¼ cup melted butter. Sprinkle ¼ cup sugar over butter, adding more if desired. Roll rectangle (wide end) into jelly-roll fashion. Using a serrated knife, cut slices 1 to 1¼-inch thick. Place cut-side up in greased muffin pans. Continue to process the other half of dough as above. Let rolls rise in warm place until double in size, at least another hour.

5. Bake in oven 10 to 12 minutes or until golden on top. Remove from oven and brush with melted butter; sprinkle with sugar. Serve warm for best taste. Yield: 2 dozen rolls.

Sally Lunn Bread

Note: *Sally Lunn cakes were originally made by Protestant refugees from France; they called them "soleil et lune." It meant "sun" for the golden color, and "moon" for the airy interior of the cake. The cake became bread enhanced by Sally Lunn, who was a pastry cook in Bath, England. This recipe goes back to 1685, and is still warm and wonderful today. I have made this bread many times for our Christian school kids to enjoy at lunch, and it helped all of them to pass their tests! It is so rich, you won't even need butter for this bread.*

2 cups flour
3 teaspoons baking powder
½ teaspoon salt

½ cup real butter
1 cup sugar
2 eggs
1 cup whole milk

1. Preheat oven to 375 degrees. Sift flour, baking powder, and salt together; set aside.

2. Beat butter and sugar together until creamy; add eggs and beat well. Stir dry ingredients alternately with milk into butter mixture,.

3. Bake in a buttered 9 by 5-inch loaf pan for 40 to 50 minutes. Serve warm plain or with apple butter if desired. Serves 8 to 10.

COUNTRY SUPPERS

"Set the Table" with Country Suppers

The following section of *Country Suppers* is filled with recipes that bring family and friends together in an informal and down-to-earth sort of way. Nothing fancy, just a big pot of **Farmer's Cabbage** or a **Favorite Meat Loaf ,** or even a big platter of **Country Fried Catfish,** all served up with your favorite side dishes and a hot roll. It's the kind of supper that a family can dig into and be themselves. The savory old-time comfort food that permeated our southern states for years is still popular today.

I can remember my first pastor's wife, Stella Guinn, bringing her famous **Chicken & Dumplings** to the annual church picnic. Looking back, the pot seemed enormous, filled with the tender rolled dumplings and cooked up in the savory chicken broth with chunks of chicken. We could hardly wait for everyone to set out their food so we could visit her table and have some dumplings. While we all wrote the recipe and vowed to go right home and make up a pot, few ever did. However, one cold winter day while my husband was at work and the kids were in school, I got the recipe and was determined to make Stella Guinn's Chicken & Dumplings. That evening when everyone settled in at the table, I started dipping up the heavenly dish. My son, Scott, ate three bowls, and to this day it is one of his favorite meals. I have been making it for my family ever since.

A country table would not be complete without the **Southern Fried Chicken,** real mashed potatoes, and corn on the cob. Country suppers are a meal in themselves and need only one or two side dishes or just a buttered roll with jelly, to make the meal satisfying. One of my favorites in this section is the **Country Beef Stew & Dumplings.** This is a savory beef stew topped with drop puff dumplings and plenty of vegetables, cooked up in a large Dutch oven. The meat is so tender and the dumplings are soft and delicious. I can assure you, there will be no leftovers.

Another old favorite is the **Roast Beef & Noodles** with your choice of **Homemade Noodles,** which are very tender and delicious, or your favorite ready-made egg noodles. This country supper deserves a beautiful table with your best country dinnerware! It will be an experience your family will talk about for a long time. Whatever you choose, enjoy it with your family, and "Set the Table" with your favorite country supper.

Rosalie's Chicken & Dumplings

Rosalie Serving Country

Rosalie's Chicken & Dumplings

Note: *This dish could be the best-loved country supper of all time. The broth is smooth and savory with dumplings that melt in your mouth. Another hit at the Country Fair, this recipe has won blue ribbons in the hearts of everyone who experiences it. Serve it up with* **Creamy Homemade Mashed Potatoes** *recipe found on page 77,* **Country Green Beans with Ham** *recipe found on page 82 and by all means don't forget the* **Sweet Yeast Rolls** *recipe found on page 113.*

1 large stewing hen or chicken

3 tablespoons chicken base,
  or 4 chicken bouillon cubes

3 stalks celery, cleaned and chopped into
  3-inch pieces

1 (10¾-ounce) can Campbell's Cream of
  Chicken Soup

½ to ¾ cup whole milk

¼ teaspoon ground black pepper

salt

1. Rinse chicken well in cold salt water and place in large 8-quart heavy pot. Cover with water and bring to a rapid boil. Skim all foam from broth as it rises to the top. When foam subsides, add chicken base or bouillon cubes and celery to broth. Cover and cook over medium heat to soft boil for 1 hour. Chicken will be tender and fall off bones. Remove chicken to large platter to cool. Remove skin, all bones, and any unsightly dark meat. Chop chicken into small pieces, then set aside and prepare dumplings.

(Time: 30 Minutes)

Rolled Dumplings

Note: *These dumplings are rolled into a large flat sheet of dough and cut into small squares. They absorb the broth and become very tender and light.*

4 cups flour

1 teaspoon salt

1 stick butter

4 eggs, beaten

½ to 1 cup Kitchen Basics
  low-sodium chicken stock

1. In large bowl place flour and salt; mix together, and work in butter until flour becomes mealy.

2. Make a "well" in middle of flour. Pour in the beaten eggs and ½ cup chicken stock; then work into dough. If dough is stiff, add a little more broth. The dough should come together soft and smooth.

3. Separate dough into 3 portions. Roll out each portion onto floured surface to a thin round circle, about ⅛-inch thick. Cut dough into 1½-inch wide pieces, and then into 1½-inch squares. Place dumplings on floured wax paper on cookie sheet in layers until all the dough has been used.

4. Remove celery from broth, and bring broth to rolling boil. Drop dumplings into broth a few at a time. Stir after each addition of dumplings. Continue to drop dumplings into boiling broth until all are used. Cover pot and softly boil the dumplings, stirring often, for about 20 minutes or until dumplings are very tender.

5. Add cream of chicken soup and milk to broth. Stir and boil gently until soup is dissolved. Add pepper and salt if desired. Add chicken and stir well. If more broth is desired, add a little more milk. Ladle soup into large bowls while still hot. Serves 8 to 10.

Chicken Pot Pie

Chicken Pot Pie

Note: *This chicken pot pie is loaded with tender chicken and vegetables cooked in a creamy sauce and topped with a flaky crust. Serve with* **Southern Salad with Strawberry Vinaigrette** *recipe found on page 65. This is meal long to be remembered. Make it up in 8 individual pie tins, pie pans, or one baking pan. Your family will love it!*

8 (5-inch) round pie tins, or 2 (9-inch) pie pans
   or a (13 by 9-inch) baking pan

3 skinless chicken breasts
Lawry's coarse ground garlic salt with parsley
½ stick butter
3 tablespoons mild olive oil

2 cups celery, chopped into ½-inch pieces
1 cup carrots, chopped into ¼-inch pieces

2 tablespoons flour
2 cups Kitchen Basics low-sodium
   Chicken Stock

1 cup frozen peas
1 cup frozen corn
½ cup red potato, unpeeled and chopped into
   ½-inch pieces, optional
½ cup frozen pearl onions, optional

1 can Campbell's Cream of Chicken soup
½ to ¾ cup whole milk
¼ teaspoon ground black pepper

1 box Betty Crocker Pie Crust mix

1. Preheat oven to 375 degrees. Rinse chicken breasts in cool water; pat dry. On large chopping board, cut chicken into 1-inch pieces. Sprinkle liberally with garlic salt on both sides. Using a large skillet, sauté chicken pieces in butter and oil about 5 to 6 minutes until no longer pink.

2. Add the celery and onion, and continue to stir-fry for another 4 to 5 minutes. Add the flour all at once, stirring into chicken/vegetable mixture until all lumps disappear. Slowly add the chicken stock and simmer for 2 to 3 minutes; mixture should be smooth and bubbly.

3. Add the peas, corn, potato, and onion stirring into the sauce. Continue to simmer on low heat for 1 to 2 minutes.

4. Add the soup, stirring it into the sauce; add the milk and pepper. Continue stirring until sauce is smooth and bubbly. Remove from heat. Makes 8 cups filling.

5. Prepare pie crust for 2 crusts according to package directions. Bring dough into a ball and flatten with your hands to make a round disk. On floured counter, gently roll out crust, periodically turning and dusting with flour. Roll dough gently to a roughly 17 by 15-inch rectangle. Cut 8 (5-inch) circles for top of pie tins, 2 (9-inch) pie tops, or trim to fit top of a 13 by 9-inch baking pan.

6. If using small pie tins or pie pans, place on cookie sheet for possible spill over. Pour filling into each pan. If using baking pan, pour all of filling into pan. Place trimmed crust over filling. Bake pies 20 to 30 minutes or until crust is a golden brown. Remove and serve while still hot. Serves 4 to 8.

Southern Fried Chicken

Southern Fried Chicken

Note: Southern fried chicken should have a golden brown, crackling-crisp coating, and be very tender and juicy inside. For best results, soak the chicken in buttermilk from 2 or more hours to tenderize, and by all means use a large cast-iron skillet to fry the chicken. Vegetable shortening will yield in a crisper chicken. Be sure to drain the chicken on a rack over a cookie sheet or pan. Keep the chicken warm in a 250 degree oven. Simply delicious!

2 quarts cool water

1 tablespoon salt

3½ to 4 pound chicken, cut into pieces

2 cups buttermilk

1 teaspoon salt

½ teaspoon ground black pepper

2 cups all-purpose flour

2½ teaspoons salt

1 teaspoon ground black pepper

1 teaspoon paprika

2 cups Crisco shortening

curly parsley

1. Preheat oven to 250 degrees. Soak chicken pieces in salted cool water for about 15 minutes to remove all blood. Rinse well and place chicken in large bowl with buttermilk, salt, and pepper. Coat chicken well. Cover the bowl with plastic wrap and refrigerate for 2 to 12 hours.

2. Remove chicken from refrigerator; drain buttermilk and rinse chicken off in cool water. In a large bowl combine the flour, salt, pepper, and paprika. Roll chicken piece by piece in the flour mixture until well coated.

3. Place a deep heavy cast-iron skillet over medium-high heat and add enough shortening to cover the bottom, about ½ inch. Heat the shortening to about 350 degrees and add the chicken pieces skin-side down in a single layer. The fat should crackle when pieces are dropped in.

4. Fry chicken uncovered about 2 to 3 minutes on each side, just enough to get a golden color, being careful not to burn. Cover, reducing the heat to medium, about 250 degrees, to avoid burning. Continue frying for another 25 to 30 minutes, turning occasionally. Add additional Crisco if oil gets low. Chicken juices should run clear when pierced with fork to ensure being fully cooked. If not ready to serve, remove chicken to rack placed over baking pan in warm oven. Continue frying rest of chicken in same manner.

5. Arrange chicken on a large pretty platter, garnished with curly parsley. Serve with **Country Chicken Gravy** recipe found on page 98. Serves 4.

Country Beef Stew with Dumplings

ountry Beef Stew with Dumplings

Note: *This is a meal in itself, loaded with chunks of tender beef cooked up in savory gravy. The vegetables are tender and the dumplings are big and soft. If you don't have time to make it when you get home from work, start it in the morning and cook it all day in the crock pot. Your family will love you for it!*

2 pounds boneless beef chuck, cut into 1-inch
    cubes or 2 pounds stew meat
Lawry's garlic salt with parsley added
½ cup all-purpose flour
⅓ cup mild olive oil

1 cup baby carrots
2 large potatoes, small quartered
2 medium onions, small quartered
4 stalks celery, cut into 1-inch pieces
salt and pepper

1 medium onion, chopped small
1 small clove garlic, minced
1 small bay leaf
4 cups Kitchen Basics low-sodium beef stock

1. Rinse meat under cool water in drainer; pat dry and sprinkle liberally with garlic salt. Dredge in flour and brown on both sides in hot oil in a large Dutch oven.

2. Add onion and garlic. Continue to stir-fry for 2 minutes. Add bay leaf and beef stock. Place lid on Dutch oven and simmer for 1 hour.

3. Add carrots, potatoes, onions and celery. Return lid to pot and simmer medium to low heat for 15 minutes or until vegetables are tender. Taste, and add salt or pepper if desired.

(Time: 15 Minutes)

uff Dumplings

Note: *These dumplings are so versatile, they can be used in any warm broth of your choice. They are so light that they will melt in your mouth.*

1 cup all-purpose flour
2 tablespoon fresh parsley, finely chopped
1½ teaspoons baking powder
½ teaspoon salt
½ cup milk

1. Make dumplings by combining flour, parsley, baking powder and salt in a medium bowl; make a well in center of flour mixture. Add milk, stirring just until moistened. Drop dough by tablespoons onto the stew. Cover and cook over low heat for 15 minutes without removing cover. Ladle in stew bowls topped with 2 dumplings. Serves 6.

Farmer's Cabbage

Farmer's Cabbage

Note: *This is a dish I created while supervising the kitchen at the Old Thresher's Country Fair. My idea was to try to celebrate the hard word of farming and the harvesting of their wonderful produce for us to enjoy. The dish was such a hit, that folks were coming back for seconds and begging for the recipe. It is great served with a hot roll, especially* **Rosalie's Dinner Rolls** *recipe found on page 109.*

6 meaty fresh country-style ribs
Lawry's coarse garlic salt with parsley added
¼ cup olive oil
1 large onion, cut into small quarters
3 medium potatoes, unpeeled,
   and cut into quarters
salt and pepper

3 cups Kitchen Basics low-sodium beef broth
1 tablespoon beef base or 2 to 3
   beef bouillon cubes

1 quart jar fresh green beans, drained or ½
   pound fresh green beans, ends trimmed
   and cut into thirds
1 quart jar fresh whole tomatoes, not drained
   or 1 (28-ounce) can whole diced tomatoes
1 large head cabbage, outer leaves removed
   and chopped in chunks
salt and pepper

1. Rinse meat under cool water; pat dry. Liberally sprinkle ribs with garlic salt. Place ¼ cup oil in bottom of largew skillet and brown meat on all sides, about 8 minutes. Add onions and potatoes and stir-fry together for 8 to 10 minutes. Sprinkle vegetables with salt and pepper.

2. Transfer meat and vegetables to a large 8-quart heavy pot. Add beef broth, and stir in beef base, or bouillon cubes. Bring to boil.

3. Add green beans and tomatoes. Add the chunks of cabbage on top of vegetables to the top of the pot. Add water to barely cover cabbage. Cover and cook over medium heat for about 1½ hours, or until meat is very tender and cabbage is limp.

4. Add salt and pepper as desired. Spoon into large soup bowls and serve with crusty bread for dipping. Serves 8 to 10.

*B*eef-Stuffed Peppers

Note: *These peppers are steeped in a savory tomato sauce making them very tender and delicious. Served over a bed of rice, this dish is a meal in itself. Even if you don't like green peppers, after tasting these you may very well change your mind.*

4 medium peppers, green or mixed
  yellow and red

1 pound ground chuck
¼ cup plain bread crumbs
¼ cup grated Parmesan cheese
2 cloves garlic, chopped
2 tablespoons fresh curly parsley, chopped
2 eggs
1 teaspoon salt
¼ teaspoon ground black pepper

⅓ cup Canola or mild olive oil

½ cup celery, chopped small
½ onion, chopped small

1 (15-ounce) can diced tomatoes,
  juice included
1 teaspoon sugar
½ teaspoon dried basil leaves
½ teaspoon salt
¼ teaspoon ground black pepper
¼ cup Kitchens Basics low-sodium
  chicken stock

1 (15-ounce) can tomato sauce

3 cups Minute Rice, prepared
parsley sprigs

1. Preheat oven to 350 degrees. Core peppers and cut each one in half. Remove seeds and ribs. Wash the peppers and set aside.

2. Mix the ground chuck, bread crumbs, cheese, garlic, parsley, eggs, salt, and pepper. Divide filling between the peppers, filling each half.

3. In large skillet over medium heat, brown the filled peppers in oil, turning once to brown, about 3 minutes on each side, being careful to keep filling intact. If all the peppers do not fit on the first browning, divide them until all are browned. Place peppers in a large deep baking dish; set aside.

4. Using the same skillet, brown the celery and onion until slightly golden, about 4 to 5 minutes, adding more oil if needed. Add the tomatoes, sugar, basil, salt and pepper. Simmer about 5 minutes. Add the chicken stock; stir until blended. Remove from heat and pour sauce over peppers in baking dish.

5. Cover with foil and bake 30 minutes. Prepare rice according to package directions. Remove peppers when hot and bubbly and arrange over the rice on a large platter. Garnish with parsley sprigs. Serves 8.

Favorite Meat Loaf

Note: *This meatloaf was one of the favorites at The Old Thresher's Country Fair. It was the featured dish on Friday, and no matter how many we made, we always ran out. For the beef base, I used Lipton Recipe Secrets, Beefy Onion, which gave the meatloaf a wonderful rich juicy flavor. Nothing fancy, just a simple recipe with great results.*

2 pounds sirloin ground beef
¾ cup plain dry bread crumbs
2 eggs
1 envelope Lipton Recipe Secrets Beefy
   Onion Soup Mix
¾ cup water
⅓ cup ketchup
¼ cup green pepper, chopped, (optional)

¼ cup ketchup for topping

1. Preheat oven to 350 degrees. In a large bowl, combine ground beef, bread crumbs, eggs, soup mix, water, ketchup and green peppers. Use your hands to mix.

2. Place meat in a lightly greased 13 by 9-inch baking pan and shape into a long thick loaf. Spread ketchup over top of loaf and bake uncovered for 50 minutes. Remove from oven and let stand 5 minutes before serving. Serves 8.

osalie's Five-Star Chili

Note: *Chili can be basic or extravagant. This chili is very basic and can be made to your liking by adding more or less spices. A great chili, with lots of savory flavor, it is very easy to cook up. Garnish with mild cheddar cheese and serve with* **Sweet Southern Cornbread** *recipe found on page 107.*

1 ½ pounds lean ground beef

2 tablespoons mild olive oil

Lawry's coarse garlic salt with dried parsley

1 small onion, chopped

1 (15-ounce) can whole or diced tomatoes, juice included

2 (15-ounce) cans tomato sauce

1 teaspoon sugar

¼ teaspoon pepper

2 bay leaves

2 cans Brooks Chili Beans, mild or hot

1 cup water

1 (1.25-ounce) packet McCormick's Original Chili seasoning mix or seasoning mix of your choice

salt and pepper

shredded cheddar cheese

2 cups cooked small shells, optional

shredded cheddar cheese

dollop of sour cream, optional

1. In large skillet, sauté ground beef in oil until no longer pink; drain oil from meat. Place meat in an 8-quart pot and sprinkle liberally with garlic salt.

2. Add chopped onion and cook for 5 minutes, until onion becomes limp. Add diced tomatoes, sauce, sugar, pepper, and bay leaves. Let mixture come to a soft boil.

3. Add the chili beans, water, and chili seasoning mix. Cover and let simmer for about 35 minutes. Add a little water if too thick. Stir chili occasionally and add salt and pepper to taste. Serve in soup bowls over small shells and garnish with shredded cheddar cheese. Serve with cornbread. Serves 6.

Roast Beef & Noodles

Note: *This dish has been served on many country tables attested by those that have a childhood memory of "beef & noodles." This particular recipe makes a large amount, which is great because the leftovers are just as good as the main course. The **Homemade Noodles** recipe found on page 131, are tender and buttery. If time is of essence, use packaged wide egg noodles.*

1 (3-pound) round rump roast

2 cloves garlic
Lawry's coarse garlic salt with parsley added
pepper
flour
oil

3 stalks celery, cut into 2-inch pieces
3 to 4 carrots, cut into 1-inch pieces
1 large onion, cut into small chunks
2 medium potatoes, cut into small chunks
salt and pepper

2 envelopes Lipton Recipe Secrets Beefy
   Onion Soup Mix
5 cups water

1 recipe **Homemade Noodles** or use
   1 package (12-ounce) wide egg noodles

1. Preheat oven to 350 degrees if cooking roast in oven. Rinse roast under cool water; pat dry. Cut garlic cloves in half and with sharp knife make 4 slits in roast in various places; push the garlic halves into the slits. Sprinkle the entire roast with the garlic salt and pepper. Dredge roast in flour on all sides. Cover bottom of large skillet with oil and over medium to high heat, sear the roast on all sides, about 8 to 10 minutes, a golden crust will form.

2. Place the roast in a large Dutch oven and add the celery, carrots, onion, and potatoes; sprinkle vegetables with salt and pepper.

3. Blend soup mix and water and add to roast. Cook roast on stove over medium heat, or bake in covered pan in oven. Cook roast for 4 hours. Remove roast carefully, so as not to break apart, keep the broth and place roast on large platter. Let cool slightly before slicing. Re-move the vegetables to a large covered bowl to keep warm.

4. Bring broth to a boil. Drop the noodles into the boiling juice and cook until tender, about 10 to 12 minutes. Slice the roast and surround with noodles. Serves 6 to 8.

Homemade Noodles

Note: *These noodles are a little fuss to make, but very rewarding in the end. If short on time, use your favorite ready-made wide egg noodles, about ½ pound.*

2 cups all-purpose flour
1 teaspoon salt
½ cup butter
2 eggs, beaten
¼ cup Kitchen Basics low sodium
   chicken stock

1. Sift flour with salt into a mixing bowl; work butter in with pastry blender until flour feels mealy. Make a well in the center; pour in the eggs and chicken stock. Combine with a fork until dough comes together; shape dough into a ball. If dough is too sticky, add a little more flour.

2. Cut the dough in half and roll out each section onto a lightly floured board or counter to a 12-inch circle. Flip often and lightly dust with flour to keep dough from sticking. Place the rolled dough sheet on a pasta rack or towel on the table. Let dough sit 20 minutes to dry (to prevent sticking when rolled up).

3. Roll up jelly-roll style and use a very sharp knife to slice dough into ¼-inch or ½-inch noodles. Toss the noodles lightly to separate and spread on lightly floured surface. Let dry thoroughly at room temperature, about 2 hours, then store in covered jars. If using immediately, drop by the handful into boiling chicken or beef broth; cook about 10 to 12 minutes, or until tender. Makes enough noodles to drop in 4 cups boiling broth.

Max, Grant, Ross, Reagan
Roman and Harpole

131

Steak Burgers
with
Onion & Mushroom Gravy

Steak Burgers with Onion & Mushroom Gravy

Note: *A hearty and wonderful way to make steak burgers, these are simmered in savory onion-mushroom gravy. This country supper will please the children as well as adults. Everyone loves a juicy steak burger covered with gravy and served with mashed potatoes. Serve with* **Creamy Homemade Mashed Potatoes** *recipe found on page 77.*

1½ pounds ground round
⅓ cup plain bread crumbs
2 large eggs
2 garlic cloves, minced
2 tablespoons fresh curly parsley, chopped
1 teaspoon salt
½ teaspoon ground black pepper
1 tablespoon Worcestershire sauce
mild olive oil

1 tablespoon butter
1 medium-size sweet onion, thinly sliced
1 (8-ounce) package sliced fresh mushrooms

1 envelope Lipton Recipe Secrets
  Beefy Onion soup mix
1½ cups water

2 tablespoons flour
⅓ cup water
salt and pepper
parsley sprigs

1. In large bowl, combine the ground round, bread crumbs, eggs, garlic, parsley, salt, pepper, and Worcestershire sauce. With clean hands, mix the meat, eggs, and spices until well blended. Shape into 6 large patties.

2. In heavy large skillet, pour 2 tablespoons olive oil and fry patties over medium-high heat, 4 minutes on each side. Remove patties from skillet.

3. Melt butter in remaining oil. Add the onion and mushrooms and sauté until the onions are golden and tender and the mushrooms are browned, about 6 minutes.

4. Blend Lipton mix and water and slowly add to pan. Bring mixture to a gentle boil. In small bowl, mix flour and water to a smooth consistency. Slowly add to gravy, stirring until thickened. Add salt and pepper as desired. Return patties to gravy. Place lid over steak burgers and turn heat to low. Simmer 8 to 10 minutes, stirring bottom of pan once to prevent sticking. If too thick, add a little more water. Serve on large platter; garnish with parsley sprigs if desired. Serves 6.

Country Fried Catfish

ountry Fried Catfish

Note: *If you like catfish, you will love this crispy fried version. The fish is very light and tender on the inside and cornmeal crisp on the outside. Marinate in hot sauce if time permits for 2 hours, or just coat and fry. Serve with* **Tartar Sauce** *recipe found on page 101 and* **Hush Puppy Patties** *recipe found on page 85.*

6 medium catfish, cleaned and dressed

1 teaspoon salt

¼ teaspoon pepper

3 to 4 tablespoons hot sauce, optional

2 ⅓ cups self-rising yellow cornmeal, fine-grind

½ teaspoon paprika

1 cup buttermilk

Crisco vegetable shortening

salt

tartar sauce and lemon wedges

Scott and Rosalie

1. Rinse catfish in cool water and drain. Place the catfish in a 13 by 9-inch shallow pan. Sprinkle with salt and pepper and add the hot sauce. Marinate for 1 to 2 hours in refrigerator.

2. Place cornmeal and paprika in a large shallow dish. Dip the catfish in buttermilk and roll it in the cornmeal until both sides are well coated.

3. In large cast-iron skillet, pour shortening to ½ inch. Fry the catfish in the hot oil (350 to 375 degrees) for about 3 to 4 minutes on each side, turning once or twice. The catfish should turn a golden brown. If browning too fast, turn heat down. Sprinkle lightly with salt during frying. Drain on paper towels. Serve catfish on a large platter garnished with lemon wedges and small cups of tartar sauce. Serves 6.

Smoked Beef Sausage with Green Beans

Note: *This one-pot supper is very tasty and so easy. Parboil the sausage to remove much of the fat, and make the dish even more appealing for those of us counting fat calories. The parboiling does not change the flavor of the sausage and still gives much flavor to the dish. For variation, use 1 pound cold-packed sauerkraut. A great country dinner in little time.*

1 pound smoked beef sausage

3 (14.5-ounce) cans green beans, undrained
   or 1 pound cold-packed sauerkraut, undrained
1 medium white potato, cut into small chunks
2 cups water

salt and pepper

1. Fill a 3-quart pot with water and bring to boil. Cut sausage in 2-inch pieces and boil for 10 minutes. Drain water and return sausage to pot.

2. Add green beans or sauerkraut, potato chunks, and water. Bring sausage, green beans and potatoes back to boil. Cook over medium heat until potatoes are tender, about 15 minutes. Add salt and pepper to taste. Omit salt if using sauerkraut. Serves 4.

Roman Harpole and Boston

CHICKEN, MEAT and FISH

CELEBRATE FAMILY

Some of my fondest memories growing up were gatherings at the family table, where Mom would serve our favorite foods and where laughter and love mingled together. Since my mom loved to entertain, we usually had family or friends over for Sunday dinners. I especially loved the holidays when Mom would get out her best china, her embroidered linen tablecloth, the pretty silverware and the goblet glasses. She would let me help her decorate and together we would make it picture perfect. All we needed was her wonderful food to make a memory for a lifetime.

For many years, my mother held all the holiday events at her home and at her table. As her family grew from children to grandchildren and to great-grandchildren, the bond of love also grew among us. How would we ever carry on without her? And yet, wasn't she preparing me all the years of my young life to continue the tradition that she established? And so we live our lives as a cycle, and I find myself loving to celebrate my own family, enjoying their presence at my own table.

As I stated in my first book, *Rosalie Serving Italian,* I still believe that food is a bridge to relationships, and it is at the family table that we bond with one another. What would a beautiful table be without the presence of family to occupy its seats? For those "special" family gatherings, this section offers wonderful recipes, such as the **Baked Ham With Pineapple Cherry Sauce** and **Roast Turkey with Cornbread Stuffing**. Both are perfect for Christmas dinner or any occasion.

Other recipes you will love for the holidays are the awesome **Standing Rib Roast** and the **Stuffed Pork Chops with Apple Cornbread Stuffing.** Both of these dishes are outstanding for flavor and appearance.

My children would love it when we would have special "family night." I would make a special dinner for no reason at all and I would let them set the table using my best china and accessories. We would light candles and gather flowers from our garden to put on the table. It was fun for them to surprise their dad with the festive dinner. One such menu included **Grilled Steaks with Thyme and Lemon.** Another time I prepared **Cajun Battered Cod** which is so good, you will make it many times over.

So, have fun and Celebrate Family; your investments will pay off not only in this life, but in generations to come.

Celebrate

Family

Rosalie Serving Country

Baked Ham
with
Pineapple &
Cherry Sauce

Baked Ham with Pineapple & Cherry Sauce

Note: *There's nothing like a beautiful baked ham studded with cloves and pineapple slices dotted with maraschino cherries. We often think this is the ultimate Easter centerpiece, and it may be, but this ham is so good, it would be a shame to have to wait once a year to enjoy it. Fix it anytime of the year for special company or just celebrate it with your own family. This is your ultimate country ham dinner served with* **Awesome Potato Salad** *recipe found on page 62 and* **Sweet Yeast Rolls** *recipe found on page 113.*

1 (10 to 12-pound) fresh bone-in ham
(I like Smithfield)
whole cloves

Basting Sauce

1 cup pineapple juice
3 cups brown sugar
2 tablespoons butter, melted

Ham Garnish

1 (20-ounce) can Dole Pineapple Slices, drained
1 (10-ounce) jar maraschino cherries, divided

Table Sauce

1 can Dole Pineapple Chunks, with juice
¼ cup whole maraschino cherries, drained
3 cups brown sugar
2 tablespoons butter
1 tablespoon cornstarch

3 fresh mint sprigs

1. Preheat oven to 350 degrees. Place ham fat side up, on a rack in a shallow roasting pan. With a serrated knife, score fat on ham into a diamond design by making long cuts about 2 inches apart both down and across. Stud with whole cloves in points of squares.

2. Make **Basting Sauce** by combining pineapple juice, brown sugar and butter. Using a small ladle, spoon some sauce over entire ham. Place ham in preheated oven uncovered on low rack and bake 3 to 4 hours or until meat thermometer registers 160 degrees. (18 to 20 minutes per pound) Do not over-bake, or ham will be dry. Baste ham every 30 minutes.

3. One hour before ham is done, remove pan from oven. With toothpicks, secure pineapple slices all over ham, and stud each center with a whole maraschino cherry. Put ham back in oven and continue to bake, basting with **Basting Sauce.** Continue to cook until time allotted for weight of ham. Remove ham from oven and let set for few minutes. Place ham on large platter. Discard remainder of **Basting Sauce.**

4. Make **Table Sauce** by combining pineapple chunks, maraschino cherries, brown sugar, butter, and cornstarch. Cook on stove in medium saucepan until mixture boils gently, about 3 to 5 minutes; mixture will begin to thicken. Place in a pretty bowl with small ladle for individual servings. Serves 12.

Stuffed Pork Chops with Apple Cornbread Stuffing

Rosalie Serving Country

Stuffed Pork Chops with Apple Cornbread Stuffing

Note: *These thick pork chops are stuffed with flavor featuring a sweet cornbread and tart apples. The combination is really a wonderful taste experience. They are also very pretty when garnished with a sprig of curly parsley and red apple slices.*

2 to 2½ cups prepared Jiffy cornbread
   muffin mix

6 bone-in pork loin chops (1½-inch thick)
Lawry's coarse garlic salt with parsley
ground black pepper
½ cup flour
oil

¾ cup butter
¼ cup onion, chopped small
½ cup celery, chopped small
2 cups Granny Smith apples, peeled, cored
   and finely chopped
½ teaspoon apple pie spice

¼ teaspoon thyme
¼ teaspoon sage
2 teaspoons fresh curly parsley, minced

red apple slices, unpeeled
parsley sprigs

1. Preheat oven to 350 degrees. Prepare cornbread mix according to box directions. Bake in an 8-inch round baking pan and set aside.

2. Place loin chops on cutting board and cut a pocket in each chop by making a horizontal cut through the meat almost to the bone. Sprinkle chops on both sides with garlic salt and pepper. Rub flour on both sides of chops. Sear chops on both sides in hot oil until crusty, about 2 minutes on each side. Remove to cutting board and set aside.

3. In medium skillet, place butter, onion and celery. Sauté over medium heat for 3 to 4 minutes. Add the apples, apple pie spice, thyme, sage, and parsley. Continue to sauté for another 2 to 3 minutes.

4. Crumble cornbread and mix into apple mixture. Stuff each pork chop with ⅓ cup stuffing mix. Place chops on a lightly oiled large baking pan. Scatter leftover stuffing around chops. Cover with foil and bake for 40 minutes. Uncover and bake an additional 8 minutes to form a crisp edge on the stuffing. Meat thermometer should read 160 degrees when inserted into the meat.

5. Transfer chops to a large platter garnished with red apple slices and parsley sprigs. Serves 6.

Meatloaf Supreme with Cheddar Potato Topping

Note: *This is the king of meatloaves, very moist and rich with a crown of creamy Cheddar mashed potatoes loaded with jewels of crumbled bacon and chopped green onions. For an impressive centerpiece for your family or friends, it just doesn't get any better than this.*

1½ pounds ground chuck

½ cup soft bread crumbs

½ cup onion, diced

½ cup green pepper, diced

⅓ cup tomato sauce

2 eggs, beaten

⅓ cup Kitchen Basics low-sodium beef stock

1 teaspoon Lawry's coarse garlic salt
   with parsley

½ teaspoon ground black pepper

Cheddar Potato Topping

8 to 10 medium red potatoes, peeled and
   small quartered

2 teaspoons salt

4 tablespoons butter

¼ cup sour cream

½ cup milk

2 cups shredded Cheddar cheese, divided

8 slices bacon, cooked and crumbled

2 green onions, tops included, finely diced

curly parsley sprigs

1. Preheat oven to 350 degrees. In large bowl, mix thoroughly ground chuck, bread crumbs, onions, green peppers, tomato sauce, eggs, beef stock, garlic salt, and pepper. Using a 13 by 9-inch lightly greased baking pan, shape meat into a loaf. Bake meatloaf uncovered for 50 minutes.

2. While meatloaf is baking, boil potatoes in salted water until tender, about 20 minutes. Drain potatoes and return to pot. Add butter and using a potato masher or ricer, mash potatoes until smooth. Fold in the sour cream, milk, and 1½ cups Cheddar cheese; fold in the bacon and green onions until smooth.

3. When meatloaf is done, spread the mashed potatoes over the top and down the sides of the meatloaf. Sprinkle the remaining ½ cup cheese over top. Broil 3 to 4 inches from heat for about 5 minutes, or until potato topping is lightly browned. With two flat spatulas, remove meatloaf to a large pretty platter garnished with curly parsley sprigs. Cut into squares and serve. Serves 8 to 10.

Roast Turkey with Southern Cornbread Stuffing

Note: *Roast turkey is great for the Thanksgiving table, but always a welcome for any special gathering. Served with my favorite cornbread stuffing, it is the best!*

1 (12 to 14 pound) turkey

1 apple, cored and quartered

1 medium-size onion, quartered

2 celery stalks, cut in thirds

2 to 3 tablespoons melted butter

salt

ground black pepper

1 cup water

curly parsley

1. **Southern Cornbread Stuffing** recipe found on page 146

2. Preheat oven to 350 degrees. Remove giblets and neck from turkey; discard or use for giblet gravy, if desired. Rinse turkey with cold water; pat dry. If stuffing turkey, lightly stuff dressing into body cavities of turkey. Close cavity with excess skin using skewers to hold skin in place. If not stuffing turkey, place apple, onion, and celery stalks in large cavity. Close cavity with excess skin, using skewers to hold skin in place. Tie ends of legs to tail with kitchen string.

3. Place the turkey breast side up in a large shallow roasting pan. Brush the skin with melted butter. Salt and pepper the turkey to taste. Pour water into bottom of pan, and use as basting over turkey during baking. Roast turkey until the meat releases clear juices when pricked deeply with a fork and meat thermometer reaches 160 degrees. Turkey should roast 15 to 20 minutes per pound. If turkey starts to brown too much, cover loosely with aluminum foil.

4. Remove turkey and let stand about 15 to 20 minutes before carving. Remove stuffing to bowl and discard apple, onion, and celery. Transfer juices to heavy 3-quart pot to make gravy. Serves 15 to 18.

Turkey Gravy

(Time: 8 Minutes)

Note: *You will love this turkey gravy made from the drippings of the roasted turkey. Double the recipe if you have 4 cups of broth.*

2 cups broth from turkey drippings

⅓ cup cool water

¼ cup flour

salt and pepper

1. Pour turkey drippings into a heavy 3-quart pot and bring to gentle simmer. In a small bowl, add water slowly to flour to make a thin paste. Slowly add the flour mixture to the broth, stirring constantly with a whisk or slotted spoon. Continue to stir gravy until thickened and bubbly. Add salt and pepper to taste. Makes 2 cups.

Southern Cornbread Dressing

Note: *This stuffing is a mixture of white bread and cornbread , and is delicious either in or out of the turkey. If using in the turkey use only a portion and the rest in a baking pan. A very moist dressing, it is great for the holidays, or anytime. Use your preference of sweet or regular cornbread, (I use Jiffy Corn Muffin Mix) and toasted bread, or your choice of herbed bread cubes. Also, I have been told that putting the uncooked stuffing in the refrigerator for an hour or overnight enhances the flavor. Either way, I'm sure you will love it.*

1 (1-pound) loaf white bread, toasted and crumbled or 1 (16-ounce) bag herbed bread cubes

3 cups prepared cornbread, crumbled

1½ sticks butter
2½ cups celery, diced
2 cups onions, diced
1½ teaspoons poultry seasoning
1 teaspoon sage
1 teaspoon salt
¼ teaspoon ground black pepper

4 beaten eggs
1 cup Kitchen Basic low sodium chicken broth
butter
turkey drippings, if available
 or additional chicken stock

1. Preheat oven to 350 degrees. Toast bread in oven or toaster and cool until hard. Crumble the bread into very small pieces and place in large bowl. Add cornbread to bread cubes; set aside.

2. In large skillet, melt butter and sauté onion and celery until translucent, about 5 to 6 minutes. Add poultry seasoning, sage, salt, and pepper and stir well; add to bread cube mixture.

3. In medium bowl, add the beaten eggs and chicken stock, mixing well. Add liquid to the dressing and toss together until thoroughly combined. Add additional seasonings if desired.

4. Butter a 13 by 9-inch baking pan and spoon in stuffing. Cover with foil and bake for 45 minutes. Uncover and baste with about ½ cup turkey drippings or chicken stock and continue to bake another 8 to 10 minutes for a golden crust. Serves 12.

ountry Fried Steak

Note: *It wouldn't be a country table without country fried steak. This ever popular meal is on almost every restaurant menu and is still considered a "comfort food." With the rich peppery gravy and mashed potatoes, this could be the perfect meal after a hard day.*

4 (4-ounce) cube steaks
Lawry's coarse garlic salt with parsley
pepper

1 cup all-purpose flour
½ teaspoon salt
½ teaspoon ground black pepper
¼ teaspoon paprika

2 eggs, lightly beaten
Canola oil

¼ cup flour used from dredge
½ cup Kitchen Basics low-sodium beef stock
1 to 1½ cups milk
salt and pepper

1. Lightly sprinkle steaks with garlic salt and pepper. In shallow dish, combine the flour, salt, pepper, and paprika. Place the beaten eggs in another shallow dish. Dredge each steak in the flour mixture, then dip in the eggs, and then dredge the steaks again in the flour; pat well to seal flour. Save ¼ cup of flour mixture.

2. Pour oil to the depth of ½ inch in the bottom of a large cast iron or heavy skillet. Heat the oil over medium high heat and fry the steaks 3 to 4 minutes on each side until golden brown. Drain on paper towels.

3. Pour off all but ¼ cup of the oil in skillet, leaving any browned bits from the bottom. Heat oil over medium heat, and sprinkle ¼ cup of the dredge flour over the oil. Stir the flour into the oil and cook for about 1 minute. Add the beef stock and stir into flour. Gradually add the milk and stir gravy about 3 to 4 minutes until gravy becomes thick and bubbly. Add any additional seasonings if desired. Place steaks on platter and pour gravy over top. Serve with **Best Instant Mashed Potatoes** recipe found on page 77. Serves 4.

Stuffed Pork Loin Roast with Apricots

Note: *This beautiful Pork Loin Roast will be the centerpiece of the table. Stuffed with wild rice, mushrooms, and pecans and served with savory gravy, you could have the mayor over and make a lasting impression. Words cannot describe how wonderful this dish is. I guess you will just have to make it.*

1 cup uncooked wild rice mix

2¼ cups Kitchen Basics Beef Stock

1 tablespoon butter

2 tablespoons butter

½ cup green onions, finely chopped with tops included

½ cup fresh mushrooms, chopped

½ cup apple, peeled and chopped small

2 tablespoons fresh parsley, chopped

3 tablespoons pecans, chopped small

2 tablespoons apricot preserves

1 teaspoon coarse sea salt

¼ teaspoon black ground pepper

⅛ teaspoon red pepper

1 (3 to 4 pound) boneless rolled pork loin roast

Lawry's coarse garlic salt with parsley added

coarse ground black pepper

1 tablespoon Tone's Louisiana Style Cajun seasoning

2 cups Kitchen Basics Beef Stock

1 cup chopped celery

½ cup chopped onion

1 tablespoon cornstarch

½ cool cup water

canned apricot halves

1 red apple, unpeeled

curly parsley sprigs

1. Preheat oven to 325 degrees. Cook rice in boiling beef stock, adding butter. Cook over low to medium heat until rice is tender, about 20 minutes. Remove from heat, and let stand about 5 minutes or until all liquid is absorbed; set aside.

2. Melt butter in heavy skillet and sauté onions, mushrooms, and apple together for 1 to 2 minutes. Add the parsley, pecans, apricot preserves, salt, pepper, and red pepper. Stir in the cooked rice until well blended; set aside.

3. Unroll the pork roast and place on a large cutting board. Slice pork open lengthwise in half, without slicing through the roast. With wooden mallet, pound the meat to flatten as much as possible. Sprinkle both sides of meat with coarse garlic salt, pepper, and the Cajun seasoning. Spoon stuffing mixture evenly over pork. Beginning with long side, roll the roast jelly-roll fashion so that the fatty side is on top. Tie with heavy kitchen string at 2-inch intervals. Arrange any excess stuffing around the roast.

4. Add the 2 cups beef stock, celery, and onion to bottom of pan. Cover lightly with aluminum foil, and bake for 3 to 4 hours, or until meat thermometer registers 160 degrees. Remove foil for the last 30 minutes of baking to brown roast. Remove from oven and place roast on a large platter. Let stand for few minutes; remove string, and cut into slices. Garnish with canned apricot halves, apple slices, and parsley sprigs.

5. Pour meat juices into a small heavy pot. If juices have cooked down, add about 1 cup beef stock. Add the cornstarch to cool water to make a thin paste. Add cornstarch water to gravy and stir until thickened, about 2 to 3 minutes. Add additional seasoning to taste. Pour gravy into gravy bowl and serve with roast. Serves 8 to 10.

Grilled Steaks with Thyme & Lemon

Note: *These steaks are mouth-watering good. Full of great flavor, they will go great with the **Potatoes with Sour Cream & Green Onions** recipe found on page 79.*

4 steaks: strip, rib eye or sirloin,
cut 1 to 1¼-inch thick

3 tablespoons fresh thyme, chopped
2 tablespoons fresh garlic, minced
1 tablespoon freshly grated lemon peel
1 tablespoon olive oil
2 teaspoons coarse ground black pepper
1 teaspoon coarse sea salt
peppermint sprigs

1. Rinse steaks with cool water; pat dry.

2. In medium bowl combine thyme, garlic, lemon peel, olive oil, pepper, and salt. Press seasonings evenly onto steaks.

3. Place steaks on grill over medium, ash-covered coals. Grill steaks uncovered, turning often, about 11 to 14 minutes for the strip and rib eyes. Cook sirloin steaks 15 to 18 minutes. Steaks will be medium rare to medium done. Check steaks by cutting through one of them during grilling for your desired taste.

4. Remove steaks to platter and garnish with fresh peppermint sprigs. Serves 4.

Sirloin Marinated Kabobs

Note: *These kabobs are marinated overnight in a lemon/oil dressing that gives the meat a great flavor, plus tenderizes at the same time. A great hit for your outdoor barbecue party that will have everyone delighted. For a crowd, simply double or triple the recipe. Can't resist this one!*

Steak Marinade

⅓ cup olive oil
¼ cup lemon juice
1 tablespoon red wine vinegar
½ teaspoon granulated garlic

1 (1¼ pound) thick sirloin steak, fat trimmed
Lawry's coarse ground garlic salt with parsley

1 large onion cut into 8 wedges
1 large green pepper, cut into 8 wedges
1 large red pepper, cut into 8 wedges
8 medium white-capped mushrooms
8 chunks fresh pineapple, optional

Vegetable Marinade

⅓ cup extra virgin olive oil
2 tablespoons red wine vinegar
½ teaspoon coarse salt
1 garlic clove, minced

4 (15-inch) metal skewers

1. Make steak marinade by combining olive oil, lemon juice, red wine vinegar, and garlic. Place in jar with lid and shake until blended.

2. Cut steak into 1½-inch chunks (makes about 20). Sprinkle liberally with garlic salt. Place meat in gallon zip-lock bag; add marinade and refrigerate over night.

3. About 30 minutes before assembling skewers, prepare vegetable marinade by placing olive oil, vinegar, salt, and garlic in a jar with lid. Shake well to blend. In large bowl, place vegetable wedges and mushrooms. Pour the vegetable dressing over vegetables to coat evenly. Let stand about 30 minutes. Do not marinate pineapple.

4. Remove meat from marinade; set aside in bowl. Remove vegetables from marinade and assemble kabobs one skewer at a time. Using a 15-inch skewer, place 5 chunks of meat alternately with one of each vegetable including pineapple chunks. Prepare a total of 4 kabobs, using all meat and vegetables.

5. Spray grill with vegetable oil to prevent sticking. Grill on gas or over hot coals about 6 to 8 minutes or longer as desired. Serve warm. Makes 4 kabobs.

Standing Rib Roast

Note: *The standing rib roast usually includes at least three ribs and is roasted standing upright, resting on its rack of ribs; this allows the top layer of fat to melt and self-baste the meat. For the elegant look of a crown, ask your butcher to cut the steaks apart into a "crown." Served with a savory stuffing and the famous **Yorkshire Pudding** recipe below, this is definitely a Sunday meal at its best.*

1 (5-pound) standing rib roast

1 tablespoon Lawry's coarse garlic salt
  with parsley
2 teaspoons coarse ground black pepper
2 teaspoons thyme leaves
  or your favorite steak rub

1. Allow the roast to stand at room temperature for at least 1 hour.

2. Preheat oven to 375 degrees. Mix together the garlic salt, pepper and thyme leaves. Rub seasoning over entire roast and place roast on a rack in baking pan with the rib side down and the fatty side up. Roast for 1 hour, and then turn off oven. Leave roast in oven but do not open oven door for 3 hours.

3. About 30 to 40 minutes before serving time, turn oven to 375 degrees and reheat the roast. Do not remove roast or open the oven door. The meat will be very tender and juicy. Serve with your favorite stuffing and the famous **Yorkshire Pudding** known to accompany this elegant roast. Serves 6 to 8.

(Time: 20 to 30 Minutes)

Yorkshire Pudding

Note: *Yorkshire pudding is a dish that originated in Yorkshire, England and is usually served as part of a traditional Sunday roast dinner. It is cooked by pouring batter into a preheated greased baking tin containing very hot drippings from the roast and baked at a very high heat allowing it to rise fast and crisp. Dipped in gravy or eaten alone, everyone should try this at least once.*

2 cups all-purpose flour   6 large eggs, beaten
1 teaspoon salt   2½ cups milk

1. In medium bowl, sift together flour and salt. Make a well in the middle of the flour and place eggs in center. Slowly whisk eggs into flour mixture until a paste forms. Gradually whisk in ½ cup milk, and then slowly add the remaining 2 cups milk until fully combined. Cover with plastic wrap and chill in the refrigerator at least 4 hours, or overnight.

2. When the rib roast is completed cooking, remove roast and set oven at 425 degrees. Using a 12-count popover or muffin pan, place 2 to 3 teaspoons meat drippings in bottom of each cup. Place muffin pan in oven and heat until very hot, about 5 minutes.

3. Remove batter from refrigerator and whisk well. Quickly spoon batter evenly into hot muffin cups. Bake for 20 to 30 minutes. Serve immediately with the **Standing Rib Roast,** while the muffins are puffy, crisp and golden brown, or, like a soufflé, they will deflate. Makes 12 muffins.

(Time: 1 Hour and 15 Minutes)

Honey-Baked Chicken over Rice

Note: *This is a great way to bake chicken with a delightful flavor of honey and curry powder. Very moist and tender with a crisp coating, this meal will definitely satisfy your family. Served over a bed of rice, the sauce flavors the rice as well.*

1 (3-pound) chicken, cut into pieces

¼ cup butter, melted
½ cup honey
¼ cup spicy mustard
1 teaspoon salt
1 teaspoon curry powder

Minute Rice, white or brown
parsley sprigs

1. Preheat oven to 350 degrees. Rinse chicken in cool water, drain. Place chicken in a 13 by 9-inch baking dish. Combine butter, honey, mustard, salt, and curry powder in small bowl; stir well. Pour mixture over the chicken and cover dish with aluminum foil.

2. Bake in oven 45 minutes. Remove foil and baste chicken with juices. Bake uncovered another 30 to 35 minutes to allow chicken to form a crisp coating. Continue to baste every 10 minutes.

3. While chicken is continuing to bake, prepare 4 cups Minute Rice according to package directions; set aside. Remove chicken from oven. Place rice on a large platter and top with chicken and juices. Garnish with parsley sprigs. Serves 4.

Barbecued Grilled Chicken with Lemon Sauce

Rosalie Serving Country

arbecued Grilled Chicken with Lemon Sauce

Note: *This is the recipe that my husband, Bill, uses every year from early spring to start of fall. It is truly a mouth-watering experience and great for any barbecue. Use chicken breasts and legs for the best grilling.*

6 large chicken breasts and 6 to 8 chicken legs
Lawry's coarse garlic salt with parsley

1½ cups olive oil
⅔ cup lemon juice
¼ cup butter

Maul's Barbecue Sauce, Original, Smoky, or Hot

1. Rinse chicken in cool water, and if time permits, let soak in 2 tablespoons of salt water about 20 minutes; drain and pat dry. Liberally sprinkle the chicken on both sides with the coarse garlic salt. Place in large pan and set aside.

2. In a 3-quart pot, place the olive oil, lemon juice, and butter. Warm on stove until butter is melted.

3. When coals are white, place the chicken on the grill and use basting brush to brush the lemon/olive sauce over the chicken. Continue grilling chicken, closing the lid over the grill when flames spark up. Every 5 minutes, and before turning chicken, brush some of the lemon sauce over the chicken. Continue to grill until the juices of the chicken run clear when pierced with a two-pronged fork, or a meat thermometer thrust into the meaty part of the breast registers 165 degrees.

4. Pour the barbecue sauce in a small pot. With same brush, baste both sides of chicken with the barbecue sauce. Close lid on chicken and let steam a few seconds. Turn chicken and re-peat the barbecue sauce and steaming about 3 times, until the chicken looks dark and crusty.

5. Return the chicken to a clean large pan and cover with foil to keep warm until serving. Provide extra sauce at the table if desired. Serves 6 to 8.

Alexandra Harpole an
Elijah Schul

rab Cakes

Note: *These crab cakes are simple to make and very delicious. Serve them alone or with the* **Sour Cream Chive Sauce** *below. Serve with* **Sweet & Sour Coleslaw** *recipe found on page 97. For the best taste, buy fresh lumps of crab meat and do not over stir the crab mixture before shaping each cake. Soft breadcrumbs are best made homemade and add density to hold the crab cakes together.*

¼ cup butter

¼ cup onion, finely chopped

2 tablespoons red bell pepper, finely chopped

1 clove garlic, minced

1 pound fresh lump crab meat, drained

1 ¼ cups soft breadcrumbs, divided

mild olive oil

salt

1 tablespoon fresh parsley, chopped

¼ cup mayonnaise

1 tablespoon Dijon mustard

1 tablespoon lemon juice

1 teaspoon Old Bay seasoning

1 teaspoon Worcestershire sauce

1 large egg, lightly beaten

dash of ground red pepper

parsley sprigs and lemon wedges

1. Preheat oven to 350 degrees. In medium skillet, melt butter and sauté the onion, red pepper, and garlic. Stir constantly until crisp tender, about 5 minutes. Mixture should be tender but not browned.

2. Remove from heat and stir in the crab meat; set aside. To make breadcrumbs, break 10 to 12 slices of fairly fresh or stale bread into chunks; grind in a food processor or blender, a few chunks at a time. Toast crumbs on baking sheet for 10 minutes.

3. Add ¾ cup breadcrumbs to the crab meat mixture, along with the parsley, mayonnaise, mustard, lemon juice, Old Bay seasoning, Worcestershire sauce, beaten egg, and red pepper; stir together just until mixed. Too much mixing will toughen the crab cakes. Shape mixture into 8 patties and dredge patties in remaining breadcrumbs. Place patties on wax paper in shallow plate and place in refrigerator for 1 to 2 hours to firm cakes before frying.

4. In large heavy skillet, pour oil to depth of ¼ inch. Fry patties in hot oil over medium heat about 3 minutes on each side or until golden brown. Sprinkle lightly with salt if desired. Drain on paper towels and serve on platter garnished with fresh parsley and lemon wedges. Accompany with **Sour Cream Chive Sauce** (see below). Makes 8 crab cakes.

Sour Cream Chive Sauce

½ cup sour cream

½ cup mayonnaise

3 tablespoon milk

½ garlic clove, minced

1 tablespoon fresh chives, chopped

2 teaspoon capers

½ teaspoon fresh lemon juice

¼ teaspoon sugar

¼ teaspoon Tabasco sauce

1. Stir together the sour cream, mayonnaise, milk, garlic, chives, capers, lemon juice, sugar, and red Tabasco sauce. Spoon over warm crab cakes. Makes 1 cup sauce.

(Time: 20 Minutes)

Cajun Battered Cod

Note: *These cod fillets are crispy on the outside and soft and delicious on the inside. For a crackling crisp coating, fry the cod in small batches. Too many pieces in the pan cool the oil and the fish can become soggy. Serve with homemade **Tartar Sauce** recipe found on page 101.*

2 pounds cod fillets

1 cup flour

1 teaspoon Tone's Louisiana Style Cajun
   seasoning

½ teaspoon salt

¾ teaspoon baking powder

1 egg, beaten

1 cup milk

flour for dredging fish, about ½ cup

Canola oil

salt

1. Preheat oven to 200 degrees. Rinse the cod gently under cool water. On a cutting board, cut the fillets into 1½ by 3-inches pieces; set aside. In a medium bowl combine flour, Cajun seasoning, salt, and baking powder. Whisk the egg and milk together well and add to the flour mixture, stirring constantly to avoid lumps. Set the batter aside until ready to dredge fish.

2. In heavy 6-quart pot, pour oil to a depth of 2 to 3 inches. Heat the oil to approximately 365 degrees.

3. Place the ½ cup flour in a shallow pie plate. Coat each fillet in flour on both sides, and then dip in the egg batter, covering both sides well. Drop the fish in the hot oil and gently hold fish down to submerge in the hot oil. Cook until the fish is done and the crust is light brown, about 4 to 5 minutes for ¾-inch thick fillets.

4. Remove the fish with tongs and place on a rack to drain. Sprinkle the fillets with salt and put the rack on a baking sheet; keep warm in the oven. Continue to cook the fillets in batches. Serve hot with **Tartar Sauce.** Serves 4 to 6.

Elijah Schultz

Orange Roughy with Vegetables & Lemon Sauce

Note: *Orange Roughy is a light mild fish that melts in your mouth. It is served with vegetables in a buttery lemon sauce, to make your taste buds jump for joy. You will definitely want to make this dish several times.*

4 (4 to 6-ounce) Orange Roughy fillets
olive oil
Lawry's coarse garlic salt with dried parsley
⅔ cup plain bread crumbs

½ stick butter
1 tablespoon olive oil
3 cloves garlic, minced
1 cup broccoli florets
1 cup thick-sliced mushrooms
½ cup thin-sliced carrots

1 teaspoon coarse sea salt
¼ teaspoon ground black pepper
1 tablespoon lemon juice
½ cup marinated artichoke hearts

1½ cups heavy whipping cream
¼ ounce Velveeta Cheese
½ cup Rope Provel cheese
    or shredded Mozzarella cheese
¼ teaspoon crushed red pepper
1 tablespoon fresh curly parsley, chopped

freshly ground black pepper
curly parsley sprigs

1. Preheat oven to 400 degrees. Rinse fish fillets gently and pat dry. Coat fillets on both sides with olive oil and sprinkle with the coarse garlic salt. Pour bread crumbs into a shallow plate and bread fillets lightly on both sides. Place fillets on oiled baking sheet and place in oven for 10 to 15 minutes or until fish flakes easily.

2. In large skillet, melt butter and olive oil together, about 30 seconds. Add the garlic, broccoli, mushrooms and carrots. Sauté vegetables until crisp tender, about 3 to 4 minutes; salt and pepper them while they are in the pan. Sprinkle vegetables with the lemon juice, using one teaspoon at a time for your taste. Add the artichoke hearts and stir in with vegetables.

3. Add the cream and bring to gentle boil, then reduce heat to simmer. Stir in Velveeta cheese until melted and smooth; add the Rope Provel or Mozzarella cheese, crushed red pepper, and parsley. Continue to stir until the vegetables and cheese are creamy and smooth; remove from stove.

4. Remove Orange Roughy fillets from oven. Place fillets on 4 individual plates and dip one-fourth of the vegetable cheese sauce over each fillet. Garnish each fillet with freshly ground black pepper and parsley sprigs. Serve immediately; serves 4.

PIES and PASTRIES

PIES, PASTRIES & PLEASURE

Feeling blue, bothered, and bewildered? Let me dish you up a piece of pie. You will soon forget your trouble and for just a few moments revel in the simple things of life—dessert. In this section, you will find just the thing to top off your busy day. There is nothing like a sweet ending, whether it is at the end of a meal, end of a meeting, or just to celebrate your accomplishments. Everyone has a sweet tooth.

For a dessert worth your highest praise, you must try the **Black Bottom Peanut Butter Pie.** Oh my, what a mouthful of bliss! This has got to be the best peanut butter pie ever, with chocolate fudge on the bottom and smooth sweet peanut butter filling on the top, then garnished with whipped cream.

Having your in-laws over for the first time? Impress them with wonderful **Bread Pudding with Custard Sauce** or maybe the best of old favorites, **Old-Fashioned Buttermilk Pie.** Both of these desserts are popular not only with country folks, but with anyone who appreciates goodness.

And what country sideboard would not boast of the best cobblers anywhere? Try the **Country Fair Blackberry Cobbler, Crusty Peach Cobbler,** or one of my favorites, **Streusel-Topped Cherry Cobbler.** These cobblers boast a flaky bottom crust, filled with sweetened fruit and topped with another crust or streusel topping. It has been said, "A piece of cobbler is a piece of Heaven."

And still, the sweetness goes on. **Rosalie's Apple Dumplings** are not only beautiful, but include the goodness of cinnamon, apples and **Brown Sugar Syrup.**

And lastly, the country folks are known for their cream pies. Thick and creamy fillings piled high with meringue, they are the show-stoppers on their tables. The favorites in this section: **Rosalie's Coconut Cream Pie, Chocolate Cream Pie,** and **Marvelous Lemon Meringue.** Make your favorite pie or pastry, and have a piece of pleasure.

Pies & Pastries

Rosalie Serving Country

elt-In-Your-Mouth Pie Crust

Note: *This pie crust is so good, you could almost eat it alone. Use it for pies, cobblers, tarts, quiches, and especially in chicken pot pie recipes. The single crust recipe makes a little more than needed, but I always like more dough to work with for a beautiful fluted high edge. Be sure to prick the bottom and sides of the pastry if baking it for cream pies; it will keep the crust from buckling.*

Recipe for Single Pie Crust
(9 or 10-inch)

1¼ cups all-purpose flour

½ teaspoon salt

⅓ cup plus 1 tablespoon butter-
flavored Crisco

4 tablespoons ice water

Recipe for Double Pie Crust

2 cups all-purpose flour

1 teaspoon salt

⅔ cup butter-flavored Crisco

5 tablespoons ice water

Recipe for Deep Dish Pie Crust
or top Cobbler Crust
(13 by 9-inch)

1½ cups all-purpose flour

¾ teaspoon salt

⅓ cup plus 2 tablespoons butter-
flavored Crisco

5 tablespoons ice water

1. Place flour and salt in bowl and mix together. Cut in Crisco until the dough resembles small peas. Sprinkle water over dough, 1 tablespoon at a time, and work in until dough begins to come together to form a ball. For double-crust pie, divide dough in half for bottom and upper crusts.

2. Roll dough with rolling pin on slightly floured surface. Using a flat turner, fold and gently turn dough over to dust with flour and prevent sticking. Continue rolling dough to fit the pie plate size. Fold dough gently in half and place in pie plate. Unfold and press into bottom of pie plate. Bake crust at 425 degrees 8 to 10 minutes for cream pies, or fill with favorite filling and bake as directed.

obbler Crust

Note: *This crust can be used for deep dish cobblers when you want a nice thick crust to top your lovely dessert. Using just half of the recipe usually makes enough for a deep slab of crust, leaving left-over dough for **Pastry Cinnamon Roll-ups** (see recipe below).*

3 cups all-purpose flour
2 teaspoons baking powder
1 teaspoon salt

1 cup Crisco butter-flavored shortening
¾ cup whole milk

1. Combine flour, baking powder, and salt in a medium bowl. Cut in shortening with pastry blender or press between your fingers until mixture resembles coarse meal. Gradually add cold milk, stirring to make a soft dough that is smooth and workable.

2. Cut dough in half and roll on floured surface, carefully flipping the dough a few times and repeating flour dusting to avoid sticking. Roll to ¼-inch thickness, shaping dough to fit over cobbler filling. Dough can be rolled to a thicker consistency if desired. Sprinkle with cinnamon sugar and bake as directed. This crust is very tender and melts in your mouth.

astry Cinnamon Roll-ups

Note: *I remember as a child hoping mom would have some leftover pie crust. I knew she would brush it with butter and sprinkle it with cinnamon. It was almost as good as the pie itself!*

melted butter, about ½ stick
Cinnamon Sugar

1. Roll remaining dough into a large circle, about ¼ inch thick. Using pastry brush, brush melted butter over entire dough circle. Sprinkle liberally with **Cinnamon Sugar** (see recipe below). Cut squares or circles about 4 inches across with pastry cutter. Roll each piece up and place on lightly greased cookie sheet. Continue until all the dough is used.

2. Bake at 400 degrees for about 15 to 20 minutes, or until tender and golden brown. Serve warm.

Cinnamon Sugar

1 cup sugar
1 teaspoon cinnamon

1. Mix together and use as directed.

Nicholas Harpole

Rosalie Serving Country

Chocolate Classic Cream Pie

Note: *This American classic is not only a favorite of the South, but of most every other cuisine. Who can pass up a mouthful of bliss like this? So easy to make and sooo good!*

1 **Melt-In-Your-Mouth Pie Crust** recipe (single) found on page 162.

¾ sugar
¼ cup plus 2 teaspoons cornstarch
¼ cup cocoa

4 egg yolks
3 cups whole milk

1 (1-ounce) square semi-sweet chocolate
3 tablespoons butter
1½ teaspoons vanilla extract

1 cup whipping cream
½ cup sifted powdered sugar
1 teaspoon vanilla

1 small chocolate almond candy bar
cocoa

1. Preheat oven to 400 degrees. Prepare pie crust and roll dough to fit a 9-inch pie pan. Prick bottom crust with fork. Flute edges and bake for 8 to 10 minutes, until golden in color; set aside to cool.

2. Combine sugar, cornstarch, and cocoa in a 3-quart heavy saucepan and stir well.

3. Beat egg yolks and milk together and gradually stir into sugar mixture. Cook over medium heat, stirring constantly with slotted spatula, until mixture thickens and bubbles. Lower heat and boil 1 minute more, continuing to stir. Remove from heat and add semi-sweet chocolate square, butter, and vanilla. Stir until well blended and immediately pour into pastry shell. Cover filling with wax paper. Let cool 30 minutes, then chill until firm.

4. Beat whipping cream until foamy, gradually adding powdered sugar and vanilla until smooth and sugar melts. Beat until firm peaks form. Spread whipped cream over filling. Using potato peeler, scrape candy bar curls over whipped cream. Sift cocoa over curls and serve immediately or keep refrigerated until ready to serve. Serves 8.

Black Bottom Peanut Buttter Pie

Black Bottom Peanut Butter Pie

Note: *Southerners love their peanuts—boiled, baked, toasted and incorporated into pies, cakes, and cookies. This is one dessert that really shows off the peanuts. The layer of chocolate on the bottom is wonderful and makes this a very rich dessert, not for the faint-hearted. Simply delicious!*

1 prepared (9-inch) Graham Cracker Crust

½ cup evaporated milk
1 cup semi-sweet chocolate chips

1 (8-ounce) package cream cheese
1 cup creamy smooth peanut butter
1 (14-ounce) sweetened condensed milk

pressurized whipping cream
Miniature Reese's Peanut Butter Cups

1 small jar Smucker's Hot Fudge Topping

1. In small bowl, microwave chocolate chips and evaporated milk for 30 seconds, stirring until chips are dissolved and mixture is smooth. Pour into bottom of prepared crust.

2. In medium bowl, beat together cream cheese, peanut butter, and sweetened condensed milk until smooth. Pour over melted chocolate in bottom of crust.

3. Using the pressurized whipped cream, make decorative dollops all around the outer edge of the pie. Next, line the inside of the whipped cream circle with the Miniature Reese's Peanut Butter Cups.

4. Place ¼ cup hot fudge topping in microwave for few seconds to thin syrup. Drizzle over whipped cream. Refrigerate pie for 2 hours or more to set. Serves 8 large or 16 small slices.

*M*arvelous Lemon Meringue Pie

Note: *The key to perfect lemon custard is to thicken the cornstarch and sugar mixture before adding the lemon juice. This lemon pie has been a favorite of my friends and family for many years. The tart lemon with sweet meringue is superb!*

1 **Melt-In-Your-Mouth Pie Crust** recipe
(single) found on page 162

1½ cups sugar
½ cup cornstarch
¼ teaspoon salt

4 egg yolks
1¾ cups water

⅔ cup fresh lemon juice
1 teaspoon grated lemon find
3 tablespoons butter

Meringue

6 egg whites
½ teaspoon cream of tartar
⅓ cup sugar
½ teaspoon vanilla extract

1. Preheat oven to 425 degrees. Prepare pie crust and roll dough to fit a 9-inch pie pan. Prick bottom crust with fork. Flute edges and bake for 8 to 10 minutes, until golden brown. Set aside to cool. Lower oven to 350 degrees.

2. Combine sugar, cornstarch, and salt in a large heavy saucepan; set mixture aside.

3. Combine egg yolks and water; stir into sugar mixture. Cook over medium heat, stirring constantly with slotted spatula until mixture thickens and boils. Reduce heat and boil 1 minute, stirring constantly.

4. Remove from heat. Stir in lemon juice, lemon rind, and butter. Spoon into pastry shell.

5. With an electric mixer, beat egg whites and cream of tartar in a grease-free bowl at medium speed until soft peaks form. Gradually add the sugar, 1 tablespoon at a time, beating at high speed until stiff peaks form and sugar is dissolved. Add vanilla, beating just until blended. Spread meringue over hot filling, sealing to edge of pastry. Brown for 15 minutes. Meringue should be golden brown. Allow pie to cool and set before cutting. Serves 8.

Marvelous Lemon Meringue Pie

Key Lime Pie

Note: *This pie is the best I have ever eaten, even in Florida. Real Key limes are sometimes hard to find, so I sometimes use regular limes that work just as well. This is a keeper recipe that you will use again and again.*

1¼ cups graham cracker crumbs
¼ cup firmly packed light brown sugar
⅓ cup butter, melted

canned whipped cream
1 lime
coarse white sugar sparkles

2 (14-ounce) cans sweetened condensed milk
1 cup fresh Key lime juice

1. Preheat oven to 350 degrees. Combine cracker crumbs, sugar, and butter and press into a 9-inch pie plate. Bake for 8 minutes; cool. Lower oven to 325 degrees.

2. In large bowl, stir together the milk and lime juice until well blended. Pour into crust. Bake pie uncovered at 325 degrees for 25 to 28 minutes. Chill 3 to 4 hours, until firm.

3. Starting at edge of pie, flute canned whipped cream to a 3-inch rim all around. Slice 1 lime into thin slices on a cutting board. Let lime slices dry slightly on paper towel, turning occasionally. Sprinkle with sugar and let dry completely. Cut slices in half, and twist to make a curl. Garnish pie with sugared lime slices. Serves 8.

Old-Fashioned Buttermilk Pie

Note: *This dream comes from Miss Aimee B's Tea Room located in St. Charles, Missouri, where I often bring friends for lunch. Amid the Victorian menu lies this mouth-watering delight. I love it just a little warm right from the oven, but it is still great the next day, kept in the refrigerator. Delicious!*

1 **Melt-In-Your Mouth Pie Crust** recipe
  (single) found on page 162

1¼ cups sugar
¾ cup buttermilk
4 tablespoons flour, heaping

3 eggs
1 teaspoon vanilla
½ cup butter, melted
1 cup coconut

1. Preheat to 350 degrees. Prepare the pie crust and roll dough to fit a 9-inch pie pan; set aside.

2. In a medium bowl, place the sugar, buttermilk, and flour. Mix together well. Stir in the eggs, vanilla, melted butter, and coconut. Fill the prepared pie shell and bake for 50 minutes undisturbed. Remove and serve warm if desired. Serves 8.

Streusel-Topped Cherry Cobbler

Streusel-Topped Cherry Cobbler

Note: *This cobbler will melt in your mouth and taste very much as though you used fresh cherries without all the work. The Streusel Topping sends this over the top. Everyone will want this recipe. Simply delicious!*

1 **Melt-In-Your-Mouth Cobbler Crust** recipe
   found on page 162

2 (1 pound 5-ounce) cans cherry pie filling

½ cup sugar

1 teaspoon almond extract

2 tablespoons butter

Streusel Topping

1 cup flour

1 cup sugar

½ cup butter

1. Preheat oven to 400 degrees. Prepare cobbler crust and place in the bottom of a 13 by 9-inch cobbler pan; set aside.

2. In large bowl, place cherry pie filling, sugar, and almond extract. Stir together until well combined. Place filling in unbaked cobbler crust. Cut butter in pieces and lay over the cherries.

3. Make **Streusel Topping** by placing flour, sugar and butter in medium bowl. Work butter into flour and sugar, using pastry blender or press between your fingers until small clumps form. Spread topping over cherries.

4. Carefully place in oven and bake for 45 minutes, or until topping is golden brown. Serve warm with vanilla ice cream . Serves 8.

Raspberry Cream Cheese Custard Pie

Raspberry Cream Cheese Custard Pie

Note: *This raspberry pie is a delightful mix between a cheese and custard filling. It is delicious either warm or cooled. The sour cream and whipped topping along with the fresh raspberries only add to the goodness. You will definitely use this recipe often.*

1 **Melt-In-Your-Mouth Pie Crust** recipe
   (single) found on page 162

2 cups fresh or frozen red raspberries

2 tablespoons cornstarch

3 tablespoons sugar

1 tablespoon lemon juice

¼ cup warm water

1 teaspoon grated lemon rind, divided

2 tablespoons butter

¼ teaspoon vanilla

1 (8-ounce) package cream cheese, softened

1 (14-ounce) can sweetened condensed milk

2 eggs

2 tablespoons lemon juice

1 teaspoon vanilla

Sour Cream Topping

1 (8-ounce) carton sour cream

2 tablespoons sugar

1 tablespoon lemon juice

pressurized canned whipped cream

¾ cup raspberries

coarse white sugar sprinkles

1. Preheat oven to 350 degrees. Prepare pie crust and roll dough to fit a 9-inch pie pan; set aside. Combine raspberries, cornstarch, sugar, lemon juice, water, ½ teaspoon lemon rind, butter, and vanilla in medium saucepan. Over medium heat, stir constantly until thick and bubbly, about 5 to 6 minutes. Pour into unbaked pie crust.

2. In a large bowl, beat cream cheese with electric mixer until fluffy. Gradually beat in sweet-ened condensed milk, eggs, lemon juice, vanilla, and remaining ½ teaspoon lemon rind. Pour cheese mixture over raspberries. Bake 35 minutes, or until set. Cheese will begin to split a little on top. Remove from oven and set aside to cool..

3. Prepare **Sour Cream Topping** by mixing together the sour cream, sugar, and lemon juice. Spread over cooled pie.

4. Flute whipped cream over **Sour Cream Topping**, beginning at outer edge and working in. Leave a 4-inch circle in the center for raspberries. Lightly cover rasberries with sprinkles. Makes 8 large or 16 small pieces.

Praline Pumpkin Pie

Note: *A great variation of the traditional pumpkin pie, this filling has a pudding-like texture with great taste and caramel topping. The candied toasted pecans make this pie a praline treat. To make this sugar-free, use sugar-free pudding, sugar-free caramel topping, and Splenda substitution for sugar.*

1 (9-inch) prepared deep dish
   graham cracker pie crust

¾ cup caramel topping, divided

1 (15-ounce) Libby's canned pumpkin
¼ cup brown sugar
¼ cup white sugar
1 teaspoon ground cinnamon
½ teaspoon ground nutmeg
⅛ teaspoon ground cloves
1 tablespoon vanilla

2 (3.4-ounce) packages Jell-O
   Vanilla Instant Pudding
2 cups whole milk
2½ cups whipped topping, divided

⅓ cup pecans, chopped
2 teaspoons sugar

1. Place caramel topping in microwave for 5 to 8 seconds to thin a little. Pour ½ cup caramel topping in bottom of pie crust; set aside.

2. In medium bowl, place the pumpkin, brown sugar, white sugar, cinnamon, nutmeg, cloves, and vanilla. Using a whisk, blend together well; set aside.

3. In another bowl, combine the pudding mixes and slowly add 2 cups milk, stirring constantly until smooth and thick. Fold in 1½ cups whipped topping. Add the pudding mixture to the pumpkin mixture and thoroughly combine. Pour filling over the caramel topping in pie shell. Spread remaining 1 cup whipped topping over filling.

4. Toast the pecans with sugar in dry skillet over medium heat, stirring constantly, about 1 minute. Sprinkle pecans over whipped topping. Drizzle remaining ¼ cup caramel topping over pecans. Refrigerate pie 2 to 3 hours. Serves 8.

Rosalie's Coconut Cream Pie

Note: *This pie is always a prize possession on the country table, and you can serve it with pride to all of your family and friends. A beautiful appearance with the toasted coconut sprinkled on top and the warm coconut inside.*

1 **Melt-In-Your-Mouth Pie Crust** recipe
 (single) found on page 162

¾ cup sugar

¼ cup plus 2 teaspoons cornstarch

⅛ teaspoon salt

4 egg yolks, beaten

3 cups whole milk

1 cup flaked coconut

1 teaspoon vanilla

1 teaspoon coconut extract

3 tablespoons butter

1 cup whipping cream

⅓ cup sifted powdered sugar

½ cup toasted coconut

1. Prepare pie crust and roll dough to fit a 9-inch pie pan. Prick bottom of crust with fork. Flute edges and bake at 400 degrees for 8 to 10 minutes, until golden in color; set aside to cool.

2. Combine sugar, cornstarch, and salt in a heavy 3-quart saucepan; stir well.

3. Combine egg yolks and milk and gradually stir into sugar mixture. Cook over medium heat, stirring constantly with slotted spatula until mixture thickens and boils. Reduce heat and boil 1 more minute, stirring constantly to avoid sticking. Remove from heat.

4. Add coconut, vanilla, coconut extract, and butter; stir into pudding until butter melts. Immediately pour into pastry shell. Cover with wax paper and let cool 30 minutes. Chill until firm.

5. Beat whipping cream until foamy, gradually add powdered sugar. Beat cream until firm peaks form. Spread whipped cream over filling. Toast coconut in dry hot skillet on stove, stirring often until coconut becomes golden. Let coconut cool and garnish top of pie. Serves 8 to 10.

Strawberry Glaze Surprise Pie

Strawberry Glaze Surprise Pie

Note: *This could be the ultimate dessert for those who love chocolate covered strawberries. Paired together with a bottom chocolate layer and cream cheese filling, this pie surprises and pleasantly delights people.*

1 **Melt-In-Your-Mouth Pie Crust** recipe
  (single) found on page 162

4 ounces semi-sweet chocolate
1 tablespoon butter
⅓ cup whipping cream

1 (8-ounce) package cream cheese, softened
½ cup sour cream
⅓ cup sugar
1 teaspoon vanilla

12 large whole strawberries

Strawberry Glaze

1½ cups water
¾ cup sugar
2½ tablespoons cornstarch
1 package strawberry Jell-O
1 cup chopped strawberries
1½ teaspoons lemon juice

1 can pressurized whipped cream

1. Prepare pie crust and roll dough to fit a 9-inch pie pan. Prick bottom crust with fork. Flute edges and bake at 400 degrees for 8 to 10 minutes. In small saucepan, melt the semi-sweet chocolate, butter, and cream over low heat, stirring occasionally until fully blended. Spread chocolate on bottom and sides of pie crust.

2. In mixing bowl, beat together the cream cheese, sour cream, sugar, and vanilla. Spread evenly over chocolate. Cover and chill in refrigerator for at least 1 hour.

3. While pie is chilling, make **Strawberry Glaze.** In small saucepan add water, sugar, cornstarch, and Jell-O. Stir together well. Bring mixture to boiling and stir until it becomes thick. Remove from heat. Add the strawberries and lemon juice; let stand until cool.

4. Dip the large strawberries into the glaze and arrange stem-end down over cooled cream cheese filling. Spread the additional glaze over pie. Keep refrigerated until ready to serve. Garnish with whipped cream. Serves 8.

Cherry Almond Pie

Cherry Almond Pie

Note: *This pie is not only delicious, but is the baker's beautiful dream. Southerners love to sport their big, beautiful fruit pies, lined up on the parlor buffet, and this could be one of the most delicious and most beautiful yet! The hot bubbly syrup oozing out of the lattice crust is just overwhelming.*

1 **Melt-In-Your-Mouth Pie Crust** recipe
(double) found on page 162

2 (14.5-ounce) cans Oregon pitted
red tart cherries
⅔ canned juice reserved
1 cup sugar
¼ teaspoon cinnamon

¼ cup cornstarch
⅓ cup cold water
2 teaspoons fresh lemon juice

½ teaspoon almond extract
¼ teaspoon red food coloring (optional)

2 tablespoons butter, cut up
Cinnamon Sugar (recipe below)

Cinnamon Sugar
1 cup sugar
1 teaspoon cinnamon

1. Preheat oven to 375 degrees. Prepare piecrust as directed, set aside. Drain cherries, reserving ⅔ cup juice in heavy saucepan; discard remaining juice. Add cherries, sugar, and cinnamon. Mix together.

2. Dissolve cornstarch in water to make thin paste. Add to cherry mixture along with lemon juice. Bring to boil over medium heat. Cook and stir until thickened and bubbly, and continue to cook and stir 1 minute.

3. Remove from heat and stir in almond extract and food coloring.

4. Roll half of pastry to ⅛-inch thickness on a lightly floured surface. Place in a 9-inch pie pan allowing edges to flow over pan. Do not trim. Add filling and dot with butter.

5. Roll out remainder half of dough on light floured surface into a 12-inch circle. With pastry cutter, cut lattice strips about ¾-inch wide and 10 inch long. Lay strips in rows over filling about ½-inch apart. Use longer strips for the center of pie and shorter strips for the sides. Fold every other strip halfway back. Starting at the center, add strips at right angles, lifting every other strip as the cross strips are put down. Continue to add strips, lifting and weaving until lattice top is completed. Trim strips even with pastry edge. Fold bottom pastry up and over ends of strips and seal. Flute edges. Sprinkle lattice strips with 1 to 2 tablespoons **Cinnamon Sugar.**

6. Bake for 45 to 50 minutes or until crust is golden and filling is bubbly. Serves 6 to 8.

Country Apple Pie

Note: *Use a deep dish pie pan for this mile-high pie. Straight from the country table, this timeless dessert is one of America's favorites. For cobbler, pour filling into a 9 by 13-inch pan. Omit bottom crust and roll pastry out in one rectangular piece to fit over top of pan. Lay over filling, sprinkle top with sugar and bake.*

1 **Melt-In-Your-Mouth Pie Crust** recipe
(double) found on page 162

6 cups Granny Smith apples, peeled and sliced
1 tablespoon lemon juice

¾ cup brown sugar
½ cup sugar
⅓ cup all-purpose flour
1 teaspoon ground cinnamon
⅛ teaspoon ground nutmeg

2 tablespoons butter
1 tablespoon **Cinnamon Sugar** (recipe below)

Cinnamon Sugar

1 cup sugar
1 teaspoon cinnamon

1. Preheat oven to 450 degrees. Prepare pie crust as directed and roll half of pastry to ⅛-inch thickness on a lightly floured surface. Place in a 9-inch deep dish pie plate: set aside.

2. Toss apples and lemon juice in a large bowl. In a smaller bowl, mix together brown sugar, sugar, flour, cinnamon, and nutmeg. Sprinkle over apples and mix together well. Spoon filling into prepared pie crust.

3. Cut butter in small pieces and lay evenly over apple filling. Roll remaining pastry to ⅛-inch thickness in a round circle. Gently fold pastry over and unfold onto top of filling. Trim off excess pastry along edges. Fold edges under and flute together with bottom crust. Cut a few slits in top crust for steam escape. Using any left over dough, cut small apple cut-outs using decorative cutters. Place 3 to 4 dough apples atop crust.

4. Sprinkle top crust with 1 tablespoon **Cinnamon Sugar.** Bake at 450 degrees for 15 minutes. Reduce oven temperature to 350 degrees and bake 35 minutes longer. Pie should be golden and filling bubbly. Serves 8 to 10.

ountry Fair Blackberry Cobbler

Note: *This blackberry cobbler was the pick of the desserts at the Old Threshers Country Fair. Served with vanilla ice cream, people would stand in line with their spoon and bowl for a serving. The large purple blackberries could be picked by the gallon on many of the farms surrounding the fairgrounds. Simply heavenly!*

1 **Melt-In-Your-Mouth Pie Crust recipe** (double) found on page 162
   or 1 **Cobbler Crust** recipe found on page 163

6 cups fresh blackberries, rinsed

1 cup sugar
3 tablespoons all-purpose flour
2 tablespoons quick-cooking tapioca
1½ cups water
1 tablespoon lemon juice

3 tablespoons butter
sugar

1. Preheat oven to 400 degrees. Prepare cobbler crust as directed; set dough aside. Rinse blackberries and place in large heavy pot.

2. Combine sugar, flour, tapioca, water, and lemon juice; pour over berries. In large saucepan, bring berries to soft boil and cook about 5 to 8 minutes, until syrup forms.

3. Place berries in a 13 by 9-inch baking pan. Add butter and fold in until melted. Roll dough onto floured counter, and make into one thick 13 by 9-inch piece. Carefully lay dough over filling. Cut slits in top of crust for steam escape. Sprinkle liberally with sugar. Bake cobbler for 40 to 45 minutes, or until golden on top and bubbly. Serves 10 to 12.

Strawberry Rhubarb Pie

Strawberry Rhubarb Pie

Note: *This pie is so good, it will literally melt in your mouth. I use more strawberries than rhubarb for sweetness but any combinations of rhubarb and strawberries can be used to total 5 cups. Fold the strawberries in last so they don't become mushy in the pie.*

1 **Melt-In-Your-Mouth Pie Crust** recipe
   (double) found on page 162

2 cups fresh rhubarb, chopped into ½-inch
   pieces or fresh frozen
1½ cups sugar
¼ cup cornstarch
2 tablespoons instant tapioca
1 tablespoon pure vanilla
½ cup water

3½ cups fresh strawberries, halved
2 tablespoons butter, cut into pieces

sugar

1. Preheat oven to 400 degrees. Prepare pie crust and roll half of dough to fit a 9-inch pie pan; set other half aside. Place rhubarb, sugar, cornstarch, tapioca, vanilla, and water in medium saucepan. Cook over medium heat until bubbly, about 5 to 6 minutes. Remove from heat and let cool a few minutes. Fold in strawberries and butter.

2. Pour filling into bottom pie crust. Cover pie with top crust and flute bottom and top crust together to make a decorative edge. Sprinkle top with sugar, and bake 35 minutes until bubbly and golden brown. Serves 8.

Crusty Sugar Peach Cobbler

Crusty Sugar Peach Cobbler

Note: *This peach cobbler literally melts in your mouth, and when served with vanilla bean ice cream, your guest with run laps around your family room. It is also easy to make this into a 9-inch double-crusted pie. Either way, it is scrumptious!*

1 **Melt-In-Your-Mouth Pie Crust** recipe (double) found on page 162
    or 1 **Cobbler Crust** recipe found on page 163

8 to 9 cups sliced fresh peaches

2 cups sugar

¼ cup flour

3 teaspoons quick-cooking tapioca

¼ teaspoon ground cinnamon

1 teaspoon vanilla

¼ teaspoon almond extract

3 tablespoons butter

sugar

1. Preheat oven to 400 degrees. Prepare pie crust, or cobbler crust as directed; set aside.

2. Peel and core peaches and slice into medium slices. Combine peaches, sugar, flour, tapioca, and cinnamon and place in large heavy pot. Over low heat, bring peaches to soft boil and cook about 5 minutes, until syrup forms. Remove from heat and add vanilla, almond extract, and butter. Stir together well.

3. Place peaches in a 13 by 9-inch baking pan. Flatten dough ball into a round disk with your hands. Roll dough on floured counter, turning and sifting flour to avoid sticking, and form one thick 13 by 9-inch piece. Carefully lay over peach mixture. Cut slits in top of crust for steam escape. Sprinkle liberally with sugar. Bake about 40 to 45 minutes or until golden on top and bubbly. Serves 8 to 10.

Rosalie's Apple Dumplings

Rosalie's Apple Dumplings

Note: *These apple dumplings are irresistibly melt-in-your-mouth delicious. A classic Southern Belle dessert, you will impress your guests with this beautiful pastry.*

Dough

3 cups all-purpose flour

2 teaspoons baking powder

1 teaspoon salt

1 cup Crisco butter-flavored shortening

¾ cup whole milk

½ cup butter, melted

1 **Cinnamon Sugar** recipe (see below)

6 small Macintosh apples

Filling

⅔ cup brown sugar

⅓ cup pecans, chopped

½ teaspoon cinnamon

2 tablespoons golden raisins

1 stick butter, divided

apple dough cutouts

Brown Sugar Syrup

1½ cups brown sugar

1½ cups water

¼ cup butter

½ teaspoon vanilla

¼ teaspoon cinnamon

⅛ teaspoon nutmeg

Cinnamon Sugar

1 cup sugar

1 teaspoon cinnamon

1. Preheat oven to 375 degrees. Combine flour, baking powder, and salt in a medium bowl. Cut in shortening with pastry blender or between your fingers until mixture resembles coarse meal. Gradually add cold milk, stirring to make soft dough; press smooth and workable.

2. Roll dough on floured surface and carefully flip the dough a few times, repeating flour dusting to avoid sticking. Roll to ¼-inch thickness, shaping into an approximate 21 by 14-inch rectangle. Brush sheet of dough with butter, and lightly sprinkle with **Cinnamon Sugar.** (You will have sugar left over). Cut dough with a pastry cutter into six 7-inch squares.

3. Peel and core out center of apples. Place one apple on each pastry square. Combine filling ingredients. Fill core of each apple with heaping 1 tablespoon filling, sprinkling some around the inner circle of the dough. Dot each apple with 2 teaspoons butter.

4. Moisten edges of each dumpling with water; bring the edges to center top of apple, pinching edges to seal. Using leftover dough, cut small apple cutouts using decorative cutters. Place 3 to 4 dough cutouts atop each dumpling. Place dumplings in a lightly greased 13 by 9-inch baking pan. Bake 35 minutes.

5. Make syrup by combining brown sugar, water, butter, vanilla, cinnamon, and nutmeg in medium saucepan. Bring to boil and reduce heat. Simmer 4 minutes, stirring occasionally until sauce thickens slightly. Pour syrup over dumplings just before serving. Serves 6.

Bread Pudding
with
Custard Sauce

Bread Pudding with Custard Sauce

Note: *This warm bread pudding will take you back to Grandma's house with memories long remembered. There is nothing like a bowl of bread pudding laced with cinnamon and raisins. Topped with warm **Custard Sauce** recipe below, one could drift away in goodness.*

3 tablespoons butter, melted

8 cinnamon rolls, iced or plain
1 quart whole milk

6 eggs, beaten
1½ cups sugar
1 teaspoon cinnamon
1 cup raisins
2 tablespoons vanilla

1. Preheat oven to 350 degrees. Spread butter in a 13 by 9-inch pan; set aside. In large bowl, place the cinnamon rolls and pour milk over rolls. Soak about 10 minutes; then crush with hands until blended.

2. In medium bowl, beat the eggs. Add the sugar, cinnamon, raisins, and vanilla; mix together well. Add the egg mixture to the cinnamon roll mixture and stir together until well blended.

3. Pour the pudding mixture into the buttered pan. Bake uncovered for 25 to 30 minutes or until pudding is firm. Let cool slightly. Spoon pudding into dessert dishes and serve with warm **Custard Sauce.** Serves 12 to 15.

Custard Sauce

⅔ cup sugar
¼ teaspoon salt
2 tablespoons cornstarch
1 tablespoon flour

2¼ cups whole milk

3 egg yolks, beaten fluffy
1 tablespoon vanilla
1 tablespoon butter

1. Mix sugar, salt, cornstarch, and flour in a 3-quart saucepan. Slowly stir in milk and cook over medium heat, stirring constantly with a slotted plastic spoon or spatula. Cook until mixture thickens and begins to boil. Boil gently for 1 minute, scraping bottom of pan to avoid burning.

2. Remove from heat. Slowly pour half of mixture into egg yolks, stirring constantly with a whisk. Blend egg yolk mixture into remaining hot pudding sauce in saucepan. Add the vanilla and butter and stir in well. Spoon warm sauce over the bread pudding.

191

Old-Fashioned Cream Puff Pastry

Old-Fashioned Cream Puff Pastry

Note: *These light cream puffs literally melt in your mouth, and can be whipped up within an hour. Serve warm with **Homemade Custard Pudding** recipe found on page 194 or use sugar-free vanilla instant pudding for those in your family who cannot have sugar. They will love you forever!*

2 cups water

1 cup butter (2 sticks)

½ teaspoon salt

2 cups all-purpose flour

8 eggs

powdered sugar

1. Preheat oven to 400 degrees. In a medium saucepan, combine water, butter and salt. Bring to a boil and remove from heat. Add flour all at once and stir with slotted spoon until flour comes together in a ball. Add the eggs one at a time, beating well after each egg to a smooth satin consistency. Drop by 3 heaping tablespoons, 2 inches apart on a large un-greased baking sheet. Add 1 tablespoon dough on top of each dollop for a "cap."

2. Bake for 40 to 45 minutes. Puffs should be well browned and hollow feeling. Cool, and with sharp knife, cut off "cap" crosswise. Remove any surface "wet" dough and keep the rest intact. Fill with the filling of your choice: **Homemade Custard Pudding** recipe on page 194 or sugar-free instant pudding. Sift powdered sugar over puffs. Makes 12 to 15 cream puffs.

Homemade Custard Pudding

Note: *This is a rich custard pudding that is great for the **Old-Fashioned Cream Puff Pastry** recipe found on page 193. This recipe needs to be doubled to fill 15 baked puffs. You can also put it in a bowl with a dollop of whipped topping and count the smiles.*

⅔ cup sugar
½ teaspoon salt
2½ tablespoons cornstarch
1 tablespoon flour
2¼ cups whole milk

3 egg yolks, beaten fluffy
1 tablespoon vanilla
1 tablespoon butter

powdered sugar

1. Mix sugar, salt, cornstarch, and flour in a 3-quart saucepan. Stir in milk slowly and cook over medium heat stirring constantly, using a slotted plastic spoon spatula. Cook until mixture thickens and begins to boil. Boil gently for 1 minute, scraping bottom of pan to avoid burning.

2. Remove from heat. Slowly pour half of the mixture into the egg yolks, stirring constantly with a whisk. Blend egg yolk mixture into remaining hot pudding in saucepan. Add the vanilla and butter and stir well. Continue to cook until butter melts and custard is thick. Cool pudding and fill cream puffs. Sift powdered sugar over each cream puff. Fills 8 puffs.

Sugar-Free Banana Pudding

Note: *This pudding is so delicious, you won't even know it is sugar-free. A wonderful dessert for all our diabetic friends, or just good for those on sugar-free restrictions. The secret ingredient of sour cream enhances the taste. Good with whipped topping, but my favorite is the baked meringue. I have added them both for your choosing.*

1 (1.5-ounce) package sugar free instant
    vanilla pudding
3 cups whole milk
¼ cup light sour cream

1 (5.5-ounce) package sugar-free
    vanilla wafers

3 medium-size ripe bananas, sliced

1 (8-ounce) container whipped topping,
    sugar-free or 1 **Meringue** recipe, following

1. Prepare instant vanilla pudding, adding milk and sour cream. Stir until thick; set aside.

2. Line bottom and sides of 8½ by 12-inch baking dish with vanilla wafers. Place sliced bananas over the wafers. Pour pudding over top. Cover with whipped topping, or make meringue. Crumble a few wafers on top if using whipped cream. Chill for 1 hour before serving. Serves 6.

Meringue

4 egg whites
¼ teaspoon cream of tartar
2 tablespoons Splenda
½ teaspoon vanilla extract

1. Preheat oven to 350 degrees. With an electric mixer, beat egg whites and cream of tartar in a grease-free bowl at medium speed until soft peaks form. Gradually add the Splenda, 1 tablespoon at a time, beating at high speed until stiff peaks form and Splenda is dissolved. Add vanilla; beating just until blended. Spread meringue over pudding, sealing to edge of baking dish. Bake for 15 minutes. Meringue should be golden brown. Cool to room temperature and place in refrigerator for few hours to chill.

Sweet Tooth Pecan Pie

Note: *What would Thanksgiving or Christmas be without pecan pie? Named Sweet Tooth because nothing can quench a yearning for sweetness like pecan pie, you will definitely use this recipe again and again.*

1 **Melt-In-Your-Mouth Pie Crust** recipe
(single) found on page 162

4 large eggs
1 cup Karo Dark Corn Syrup
1 cup sugar
⅓ cup butter, melted
pinch of salt
1½ teaspoons vanilla

1½ cups pecans

whipped cream for garnish, optional

1. Preheat oven to 350 degrees. Prepare pie
   crust and roll dough to fit a 9-inch pie pan.
   Flute edges and set aside.

2. In large bowl, beat eggs until frothy. Add the corn syrup, sugar, melted butter, salt and vanilla. Continue to whisk gently until all ingredients are well combined.

3. Add the pecans and fold into syrup mixture. Pour into unbaked pie crust. Pecans should surface to the top. Bake for 50 minutes. Pie is done when surface of pie springs back when lightly tapped. Garnish with fluted whipped cream if desired. Serves 8.

Vanilla Torte

Note: *This torte is one of my son Scott's, favorite desserts. Made by his mother-in-law and my friend, Kathie Hut-tegger, it is a must at most family gatherings. The crust is rich with brown sugar and pecans, and the filling is layered with cream cheese and pudding. Delicious!*

Crust

1¼ cups flour
1 tablespoon brown sugar
6 tablespoons butter
½ cup chopped pecans

Layer 1

1 (8-ounce) package cream cheese
1 cup confectioners' sugar
1 (16-ounce) container Cool Whip, divided

Layer 2

1 (3.9-ounce) package Jell-O instant
    vanilla pudding mix
1½ cups milk

Layer 3

1 (3.9-ounce) package Jell-O instant
    chocolate pudding mix
1½ cups milk

Layer 4

remaining cool whip
½ cup chopped pecans
chocolate curls, optional

1. Preheat oven to 350 degrees. In medium bowl prepare crust by mixing together flour and brown sugar. Cut in butter until crumbly and stir in pecans. Press into a glass 13 by 9-inch baking dish and bake 15 minutes. Remove from oven and allow to cool.

2. Prepare layer 1 by beating together cream cheese and powdered sugar with electric mixer until smooth. Fold in ½ container of Cool Whip until well blended. Spread onto cooled crust.

3. Prepare layer 2 by mixing the vanilla pudding mix into milk, stirring together just until blended. Pour over cream cheese layer immediately so that pudding can thicken in an even measure. Allow several minutes to set.

4. Prepare layer 3 by mixing the chocolate pudding mix into the milk and stirring just until blended. Pour over vanilla pudding, waiting until pudding is set before continuing.

5. After puddings have set, top with remaining half container of Cool Whip. Sprinkle top with chopped pecans, and garnish with chocolate curls if desired. Makes 20 servings.

CAKES, COOKIES & CANDIES

This section, *Cakes, Cookies & Candies,* comprises some of the most beautiful cakes, yummy cookies and prized candies of country life and southern states. It has been said that no one can make the beautiful three-layer stately cakes as can the ladies of the South— cakes that win blue ribbons at the country fairs, such as **Rosalie's Blue Ribbon Carrot Cake, Lemon Coconut Cake with Lemon Curd Filling,** and the beautiful **Red Velvet Cake Supreme.** These cakes stand tall on cake plates and are works of art as well as incredibly delicious. I have seen them used as the centerpiece of the table instead of flowers or candle arrangements, catching the eye of everyone entering the room.

Country ladies also pride themselves in their pound cakes. Made with plenty of butter and eggs, they are rich, smooth, and dense with flavor. Be sure to try the **Cream Cheese Pound Cake with Strawberries.** Another old favorite is the **German Chocolate Cake with Coconut Pecan Frosting,** rich with flavor from the inside out.

Cheesecakes are also a specialty of the country cuisine. Every Christmas my family's favorite is **Sheraton's Famous Cheesecake with Pineapple Topping.** However, I must mention the **Pumpkin Swirl Cheesecake with Toasted Candied Walnuts,** and the awesome **Turtle Dove Cheesecake.** These cheesecakes are smooth and rich and will definitely become the highlight of the meal.

Cookies are also a favorite in this section and some favorites are: **Sugared Pecan Balls, Almond Crescents,** and **Chocolate Covered Cherry Cookies.**

To say that candy is a common commodity of the country folks is an understatement. Homemade candy is sported on platters and passed around at teas and luncheons right along with the other desserts. One of the most popular is **Honeycomb Peanut Brittle.** This peanut brittle will not hurt your teeth because it has a foamy honeycomb texture that will literally melt in your mouth. Do also try the famous **Creamy Marshmallow Fudge** and **Heavenly Hash.**

Rosalie Serving Country

Cakes, Cookies, & Candies

Rosalie Serving Country

Cream of Coconut Cake

Rosalie Serving Country

Cream of Coconut Cake

Note: *This cake is very moist and luscious and has the similarity of pudding cake. Topped with whipped topping and soft grated coconut, the flavor of cream and coconut is enjoyed from top to bottom.*

butter
flour

1 Duncan Hines Moist Deluxe Classic White cake mix
3 large eggs
1⅓ cups water
¼ cup mild olive oil
1 teaspoon coconut extract

1 can cream of coconut
1 can sweetened condensed milk

1 (16-ounce) container Cool Whip
1 cup shredded coconut

1. Preheat oven to 350 degrees. Butter a 13 inch by 9-inch cake pan and dust with flour.

2. Combine cake mix; eggs, water, oil, and extract. Mix cake by hand just until blended. Pour batter into cake pan and spread out evenly. Bake for 28 to 30 minutes, or until cake bounces back when touched.

3. In a medium bowl, combine the cream of coconut and the condensed milk; stir together until blended. While cake is still warm, poke holes all over the cake using a fork. Pour the coconut/milk mixture over top of cake, letting it seep down through the holes. Let stand for a few minutes until cooled.

4. Spread whipped topping over top of cake and sprinkle with coconut. Keep refrigerated. Makes 12 servings.

Lemon Coconut Cake with Lemon Curd Filling

Note: *This 3-layer beauty is tall, stately and scrumptious! You will need to double the recipe to get 3 layers, with batter left over for cupcakes. The **Lemon Cream Cheese Frosting** recipe found on page 205 will frost 2 cakes and leave plenty enough left over to frost cupcakes when doubling the recipe. The **Lemon Curd** recipe found on page 204 is outstanding and the best one I have ever come across. This is a cake to be handed down from generation to generation!*

butter

flour

1 Duncan Hines Moist Deluxe Lemon cake mix

1 (3.9-ounce) package Jell-O instant lemon pudding mix

3 large eggs

1 ⅓ cup water

⅓ cup freshly squeezed lemon juice

½ cup mild olive oil

1 tablespoon freshly grated lemon peel

1 teaspoon lemon extract

1 teaspoon butter extract

1 recipe **Lemon Curd Filling**

1 recipe **Lemon Cream Cheese Frosting**

1 cup shredded coconut

maraschino cherries

1. Preheat oven to 350 degrees. In large bowl combine cake and pudding mixes; stir together with a whisk.

2. Add eggs, water, lemon juice and oil. Stir mixture by hand; do not over mix.

3. Using grater, scrape lemon to make 1 tablespoon lemon peel. Add grated lemon peel to batter, along with lemon and butter extracts. Fold in gently until well mixed.

4. Repeat steps 1, 2, and 3 to make enough batter for 3 cake pans. Use leftover batter to fill one large (6-cup) cupcake pan.

5. Bake cakes for 28 to 30 minutes; cakes may slightly crack on top. Remove cakes to a cake rack and let cool 10 minutes. Flip pans over to remove cakes, and let cakes completely cool on wire rack until ready to frost. Bake cup cakes 15 to 18 minutes.

6. Prepare **Lemon Curd Filling** and frost cake with **Lemon Cream Cheese Frosting** (as follows).

To assemble cake:

1. Using a pedestal cake plate, cover plate edges with waxed paper strips to catch coconut as it is patted on cake. Remove after decorating cake.

2. Place one layer of cake top-side down on the cake plate. Cover with ½ cup lemon curd. Place second layer top-side down over lemon curd. Cover second layer with ½ cup lemon curd. Place third layer top-side up over second layer. Insert a wooden bamboo stick or skewer through the center of all three layers to hold the cake in place while frosting cake.

3. With bamboo stick in place, frost top and sides of cake with the **Lemon Cream Cheese Frosting.** Spread about ⅓ of the lemon curd over frosting on top of cake within 1 inch of rim.

4. Pat coconut from your hand onto sides of cake. Garnish top of cake with coconut, letting some of the yellow lemon curd peek through coconut to give a beautiful "yellow glow" to top of cake. Remove waxed paper from under cake and remove bamboo stick when cake is steady. Garnish top of cake with 3 large maraschino cherries. Serves 12 to 16 .

203

Lemon Curd

Note: *This awesome clear lemon filling is beautiful to look at and addicting when tasted. Truly a must in Country or Southern cuisine, lemon curd can be used for fillings in pound cakes, cup cakes, over crépes, and in lemon bread puddings. Cook in the top of a double broiler or heat-proof bowl that will fit snugly over the saucepan. Use this for the filling in the* **Lemon Coconut Cake with Lemon Curd Filling** *recipe found on page 202.*

1 double boiler

3 eggs
¾ cup sugar
⅓ cup freshly squeezed lemon juice
1 tablespoon finely grated lemon zest
6 tablespoons cold butter

1. Fill bottom of double boiler pan with 3 inches water. Bring to boil.

2. In top pot of double broiler, or bowl, combine the eggs, sugar, lemon juice, and lemon zest. Begin stirring mixture over the boiling water with slotted spoon or whisk; continue for 8 to 10 minutes. The mixture will thicken to a bright yellow satin consistency. Remove from heat and stir in the butter a few tablespoons at a time, stirring until melted.

3. Cool the lemon curd, and use over layers and top of the **Lemon Coconut Cake with Lemon Curd Filling.** This lemon curd can be stored in a glass jar for up to 2 weeks in the refrigerator. Makes 2 cups.

Lemon Cream Cheese Frosting

Note: *This frosting is wonderful over the **Lemon Coconut Cake with Lemon Curd Filling,** recipe found on page 202. The recipe makes a large amount with plenty left over for another cake or cupcakes; it can also be stored in an air-tight container for up to 2 weeks. A delicious frosting that can be changed easily by replacing the lemon juice with orange, kiwi, or pineapple juice.*

2 (8-ounce) packages cream cheese, softened

1 stick butter

5 cups powdered sugar

¼ cup freshly squeezed lemon juice

2 teaspoons freshly grated lemon zest

1½ teaspoons vanilla

1. Cream cheese and butter in large bowl with electric mixer. Gradually add the powdered sugar, adding a little lemon juice after each addition. Continue to mix until smooth.

2. Before last addition of powdered sugar, add the lemon zest and vanilla. Complete mixing until blended in. Do not over mix frosting or it will become too thin. Makes 4 cups.

Pineapple Upside-Down Cake

Note: *Pineapple Upside-Down Cake has been a favorite for all time. I have used it on my catering list for as long as I can remember because it was one of the most requested desserts. The pecans caramelize into the syrup, adding a little crunch. Don't shy from the olive oil; it gives the cake a wonderful flavor.*

1 Pillsbury Moist Supreme yellow cake mix

1 cup water

⅓ cup mild olive oil

3 eggs

½ stick butter, melted

2 cups light brown sugar

1 (20-ounce) can pineapple slices or chunks, drained

8 to 10 maraschino cherries

½ cup whole pecans

1. Preheat oven to 350 degrees. In large bowl, mix by hand the cake mix, water, oil, and eggs, just until all lumps are dissolved. Do not over-mix.

2. Coat the bottom of a 13 by 9-inch baking pan with butter. Add the brown sugar and spread evenly over the butter. Arrange the drained pineapple slices or chunks over the brown sugar. Place a maraschino cherry in the center of each pineapple ring. If using chunks, cut some of the big chunks in half and place the cherries in various places around the chunks. Place the pecans around the pineapples. Pour the cake batter over all.

3. Bake for 35 minutes or until middle of cake springs back. Remove cake from oven. Loosen sides of cake with a spatula. Place a large cookie sheet over the cake and using both hands with pot-holders, flip the cake over onto the cookie sheet. Be sure to hold the cookie sheet steady over the cake pan while flipping. Serve warm or at room temperature. Makes 12 slices.

Red Velvet Cake Supreme

Note: *This grand beauty is the top of the line for Red Velvet Cakes. From the rich chocolate cake to the coconut cream-filled layers, all topped off with the sugar coated pecans; goodness just oozes out all over the place. So beautiful and stately, you could use it for any special occasion!*

butter

cocoa

10 tablespoons butter

1⅔ cups sugar

2 eggs

1 (1-ounce) bottle red liquid food coloring

1 square Baker's semi-sweet baking chocolate, melted

2 cups sifted cake flour

¼ cup Hershey's cocoa

½ teaspoon salt

1 teaspoon baking soda

1 cup plus 2 tablespoons buttermilk

2 teaspoons white vinegar

2 tablespoons vanilla

2 egg whites

Cream Cheese Frosting

2 (8-ounce) packages cream cheese

1 stick butter

4 cups confectioners' powdered sugar

2 teaspoons vanilla

Filling & Topping Garnish

2 cups soft shredded coconut

1 cup toasted candied pecans, left whole

3 large maraschino cherries, with stems

pressurized canned whipped cream

1. Preheat oven to 350 degrees. Butter 3 (9-inch) cake pans and dust with Hershey's dark unsweetened cocoa.

2. In mixing bowl, cream butter and sugar until fluffy. Add eggs, and continue to beat until smooth.

3. Add the food coloring and melted chocolate (melt chocolate slowly in microwave); beat on low until well blended.

4. In medium bowl, combine cake flour, cocoa, salt, and baking soda; mix well. In a 2-cup measuring bowl, combine buttermilk and vinegar. Alternately beat dry ingredients and buttermilk mixture into creamed mixture until smooth. End with dry mixture. Stir in vanilla.

5. Beat egg whites in a small bowl until stiff peaks form; fold into batter. Pour batter into prepared pans. Bake 25 to 28 minutes until cake bounces back when touched.

6. Cool cakes in pans for about 10 minutes, and then turn onto wire rack sprayed with cooking spray. Let cool completely.

7. Make cream cheese frosting by combining cream cheese with butter in mixing bowl. Beat until smooth; add powdered sugar 1 cup at a time and continue beating until mixture is satin-smooth. Add vanilla and stir in well. Frost layers, sides and top of cake (see below).

8. Place coconut in medium bowl; set aside. Sprinkle pecans with 1 tablespoon sugar and toast in skillet over medium heat about 2 to 3 minutes. Sugar will melt and pecans will become fragrant and toasted. Remove to waxed paper to cool; set aside.

To assemble cake:

1. Place first layer of cake top-side down on cake stand and cover with liberal amount of frosting. Sprinkle layer with ¼ cup coconut. Place second layer top-side down over coconut and repeat frosting; sprinkle with coconut. Place third layer top-side up over coconut and frost top and sides of cake, using remaining frosting. Sprinkle remaining coconut on top and sides of cake. Use more coconut if needed.

2. Spread the pecans over the coconut on top layer. In center of top layer, place 3 maraschino cherries with stems. Flute the whipped cream around the bottom and top of cake, if desired. Serves 12 to 16.

207

German Chocolate Cake

Note: *This cake will knock the socks off your feet, it is so delicious. If you like German chocolate cake, this one is the best. Together with the **Coconut Pecan Frosting** and the rich chocolate flavor, this cake will win most any contest.*

butter

flour

1 cup buttermilk

1 teaspoon baking soda

1 cup butter

2 cups sugar

4 egg yolks

1 (4-ounce) package Baker's German
   Sweet Chocolate

½ cup boiling water

1 teaspoon vanilla

2¼ cups cake flour

¼ teaspoon salt

4 egg whites

1 **Coconut Pecan Frosting** recipe
   on page 210

1. Preheat oven to 350 degrees. Butter and flour three 9-inch cake pans; shake off excess flour. Combine buttermilk and baking soda in a two-cup measure to allow room for mixture to foam up; set aside.

2. Cream butter and sugar with electric mixer until fluffy and light. Add egg yolks one at a time and beat well after each addition; set mixture aside. Place chocolate in boiling water and stir to melt; add vanilla and blend with chocolate until smooth. Add to sugar/butter mixture and with electric mixer, blend together.

3. Combine flour and salt. Add to batter alternately with buttermilk mixture, ending with flour.

4. Clean beaters and beat egg whites until stiff. Gently fold egg whites into batter. Pour batter evenly into prepared cake pans. Bake 30 minutes, or until cake springs back when lightly touched. Remove cakes from oven and cool 10 minutes on wire racks. Gently run butter knife around each cake and invert cakes onto racks sprayed with cooking spray. Let cool completely.

5. Prepare **Coconut Pecan Frosting.** Place first layer of cake on pedestal cake platter top-side down and frost; repeat with second layer. Place third layer top-side up and complete frosting sides and top of cake. Serves 12.

German Chocolate Cake

Coconut Pecan Frosting

Note: *This frosting is rich and smooth loaded with coconut and pecans. Used mostly for **German Choco-late Cake** recipe found on page 208, it can also be used as a sauce as well as frosting. Delicious!*

4 egg yolks
1 (12-ounce) can evaporated milk
1½ teaspoon vanilla
1½ cup sugar
¾ cup butter

1 cup sweet shredded coconut
1½ cups pecans, coarsely chopped, and
   toasted
2 teaspoons sugar

1 large maraschino cherry

1. In large saucepan, combine egg yolks, milk, and vanilla; beat with wire whisk until blended. Add the sugar and butter, then cook over medium heat 12 minutes or until thickened and golden brown; stirring constantly. Remove from heat.

2. Toast the pecans in dry skillet with sugar added, stirring constantly, 3 to 4 minutes or until nuts become aromatic and toasted. Remove to wax paper; let cool. Add the coconut and pecans to saucepan with frosting and mix well. Cool to desired spreading consistency. Frost between layers and top of cake. Garnish top with maraschino cherry in the center.

Heath Bar Chocolate Cake

Note: *This cake is rich in chocolate, and the goodness of caramel and heath bits will send it over the top. A wonderful treat for any special occasion, or just to surprise your family—you will be the praised mother!*

butter
flour

1 Duncan Hines Moist Deluxe Devil's Food cake mix
3 large eggs
½ cup mild olive oil
1½ cups water

1 can sweetened condensed milk
1 (12.25-ounce) jar Smucker's Caramel Topping

1 large container Cool Whip
3 Heath Candy Bars, crumbled

1. Preheat oven to 350 degrees. Butter a 13 by 9-inch cake pan and dust with flour.

2. In large bowl, combine cake mix with eggs, oil, and water. Stir by hand until all ingredients are well combined and batter is mostly smooth. Pour batter into floured pan and bake for 28 to 30 minutes, or until cake bounces back to touch.

3. Remove cake from oven and place on rack. While cake is still warm, poke holes all over top and down through cake with large fork. Pour the condensed milk over top of cake, then pour the caramel topping over the cake.

4. Let the cake cool completely and frost with Cool Whip. Crumble candy bars over the cool whip. Keep cake cool until served. Serves 12.

lack Forest Cake

Note: *This cake is pure chocolate delight layered with a rich fudge icing and cherry pie filling. Garnish sides and top with whipped cream and cake crumbs for an elegant look. Standing tall on your pedestal cake platter, you could enter this cake at the country fair.*

butter

cocoa

1 Duncan Hines Moist Deluxe Devil's Food
 cake mix
1 (3.9-ounce) package Jell-O instant
 chocolate pudding

3 large eggs
½ cup mild olive oil
1½ cups water
1 teaspoon cherry extract
½ teaspoon almond extract

Chocolate Fudge Icing

2 cups sugar

⅔ cup evaporated milk

½ cup butter

1 cup semisweet chocolate chips

½ teaspoon cherry extract

1 teaspoon vanilla

1 (1 pound 5-ounce) can cherry pie filling

3 cups heavy whipping cream
⅓ cup sifted powdered sugar

1. Preheat oven to 350 degrees. Butter two 9-inch cake pans and dust with cocoa; set aside. In large mixing bowl combine cake and pudding mixes; stir together.

2. Add the eggs, oil, water, cherry extract and almond extract. Mix by hand until thoroughly blended. Do not over mix. Divide the batter between the two cake pans. Bake cakes for 28 to 30 minutes. Cakes may crack on top, which is normal, and should spring back when lightly touched. Remove cakes from oven and let cool on rack about 10 minutes. Spray cake rack with cooking spray and flip cakes onto rack to cool completely.

3. Make **Chocolate Fudge Icing** by placing sugar and evaporated milk in a 2-quart saucepan. Add the butter and cook over low heat, stirring to dissolve the sugar and melt the butter. Increase the heat just enough to bring the mixture to a boil. Let boil for 2 minutes. Remove from heat and add the chocolate chips, beating until smooth. Stir in the cherry extract and vanilla. Let frosting set about 10 minutes to thicken while the cakes are cooling.

4. Cover edges of a pedestal cake plate with waxed paper strips to catch cake crumbs. The paper can be removed easily after decorating the cake. With sharp serrated knife, cut each cake layer horizontally making 4 layers. Crumble one of the cake layers to make fine crumbs for garnishing sides of cake.

5. Place one cut layer of cake on the cake plate. Spread chocolate icing on first layer, then spread ¾ cup cherry pie filling over frosting. Repeat process with second layer. Place the top layer top-side up over the second layer. Place a wooden bamboo stick or skewer down through the center of layers to hold the cake in place while completing icing the cake. Ice the top with remaining icing and place the rest of the cherry filling over the middle of the top layer, leaving an inch rim around cake for the pressurized whipped topping to garnish.

6. Beat whipping cream until foamy; gradually add the powdered sugar, beating until stiff peaks form. Spread the whipped cream in a thick layer over sides and up to top rim of the cake. Pat the fine cake crumbs around the sides of the cake onto the whipped cream. With the pressurized whipped cream, flute cream around top rim of cake and surrounding cherries. Remove bamboo stick or skewer. Cool in refrigerator until ready to serve. Serves 12 to 16.

Elijah, Dana and Sebastian Schultz

213

Banana Supreme Cake with Candied Walnuts

Note: *If you like bananas, you will love this cake. A very moist dense cake with a crunchy bite of candied walnuts makes this is a blue ribbon special. Kept in a closed cake container, this cake will last several days. Frost with* **Banana Cream Coconut Frosting** *recipe found on page 217.*

butter

flour

1 cup butter, softened

3 cups sugar

3 large bananas

1 tablespoon lemon juice

4 eggs, beaten

3¾ cups all-purpose flour

2 teaspoons baking soda

1 cup buttermilk

2 teaspoons vanilla extract

1 teaspoon butter extract

2 tablespoons freshly squeezed orange juice

1 cup walnuts, chopped

1 tablespoon brown sugar

1 recipe **Banana Cream Coconut Frosting**

Toasted Candied Walnuts

⅔ cup walnuts

1 tablespoon brown sugar

1. Preheat oven to 350 degrees. Butter and lightly flour three 9-inch round cake pans. In large mixing bowl, cream butter and sugar with electric mixer. In small bowl, cut bananas in small chunks and sprinkle with lemon juice. Add to butter mixture; mix on low setting until smooth, stir in the eggs.

2. In another bowl, combine the flour and baking soda; mix together. Add to banana mixture alternately with buttermilk, beginning and ending with flour mixture. Blend together well after each addition. Add the vanilla, butter extract, and orange juice.

3. In small skillet, combine walnuts and sugar. Toast nuts over medium heat until browned and aromatic, about 2 to 3 minutes. Remove and fold into batter.

4. Divide the batter between the 3 cake pans. Bake for 35 to 40 minutes or until a wooden toothpick in center comes out clean. Remove from oven and place cakes on wire racks for 10 minutes to cool. Spray cake racks with cooking spray and flip cakes out onto racks, cooling completely until ready to frost.

5. Prepare **Banana Cream Coconut Frosting** and frost cakes as follows.

Banana Supreme Cake with Candied Walnuts recipe
continued on page 217

Banana Supreme Cake with Candied Walnuts

Elijah and Sebastian Schultz

Rosalie Serving Country

Banana Supreme Cake with Candied Walnuts recipe continued from page 214

To Assemble Cake:

1. On a pedestal or round cake plate, place one layer of cake top-side down. Spread about ⅓ cup frosting over first layer. Place second layer top-side down over frosting and frost with another ⅓ cup. Place third layer top-side up over second layer. Place a wooden bamboo stick or skewer down through the center of layers to hold the cake in place while completing frosting cake. Using remaining frosting, frost sides and top of cake.

2. Arrange walnuts on top of cake in a wide circle.

3. Remove bamboo stick when cake is frosted. Garnish with a large-stemmed maraschino cherry. Serves 12 to 16.

(Time: 10 Minutes)

Banana Cream Coconut Frosting

1 cup mashed bananas
2 teaspoons lemon juice

½ cup butter, softened
1 (8-ounce) package cream cheese
1 teaspoon vanilla
4 cups powdered sugar

1 cup flaked coconut, toasted

⅔ cup chopped walnuts
1 tablespoon brown sugar

1 large maraschino cherry for garnish

1. Combine mashed bananas and lemon juice; set aside.

2. With an electric mixer or food processor, cream softened butter and cream cheese at medium speed until combined. Add the bananas and vanilla to cream cheese mixture. Add powdered sugar a little at a time and continue to mix with banana mixture until smooth; stir in the coconut.

3. In small skillet, combine walnuts and sugar. Toast nuts over medium heat until browned and aromatic, about 2 to 3 minutes. Remove and let cool on waxed paper.

217

Chocolate Sour Cream Cake

Note: *This cake is so rich and moist, to add frosting is almost redundant. Just a sprinkle of powdered sugar is really all you need. Serve warm right out of the oven with vanilla ice cream.*

cooking spray
flour

1 box (18.25-ounce) plain Duncan Hines
  Moist Deluxe Devil's Food cake mix
1 package (3.9-ounce) chocolate instant pudding mix
4 large eggs
1 cup sour cream
½ cup water
½ cup mild olive oil

1½ cups semisweet chocolate chips
powdered sugar

1. Preheat oven to 350 degrees. Spray a 12-cup Bundt pan lightly with vegetable oil and dust with flour. Shake off excess flour, and set pan aside.

2. Place the cake mix, pudding mix, eggs, sour cream, water, and oil in a large mixing bowl. Blend with an electric mixer on low speed for 1 minute. Stop the machine and scrape down the sides of the bowl with a rubber spatula. Increase the mixer speed to medium and beat 2 more minutes. Scrape down sides of bowl and fold in the chocolate chips. Batter will be thick. Evenly spoon batter into the pan; place on middle rack in oven.

3. Bake the cake until it springs back when lightly pressed with your finger, about 45 to 50 minutes. Remove pan from oven and place on wire rack to cool for 20 minutes. Run a long sharp knife around the edge of the cake and invert onto large cake platter. Dust cake with powdered sugar. Serve warm with ice cream if desired. Serves 12.

Maple Sugar Syrup Cake

Note: *The pure maple syrup coupled with candied walnuts, make this dessert absolutely delicious! Don't fudge on the syrup, make sure it is pure maple.*

butter

flour

2¼ cups all-purpose flour

2 teaspoons baking powder

½ teaspoon baking soda

½ teaspoon salt

½ teaspoon ground ginger

¼ teaspoon cinnamon

½ cup hot water

½ cup butter

½ cup sugar

1 egg

1 egg yolk

1 teaspoon butter extract

1 cup pure maple syrup

Maple Syrup Icing

1½ cups powdered sugar, divided

2 tablespoons softened butter

¼ cup pure maple syrup

3 teaspoons milk

1 teaspoon vanilla

Toasted Walnuts

¾ cup walnuts, coarsely chopped

2 tablespoons brown sugar

1. Preheat oven to 350 degrees. Butter and flour Bundt pan; set aside. In medium bowl, combine flour, baking powder, baking soda, salt, ginger, and cinnamon; set aside.

2. In large mixing bowl, beat butter and sugar with electric mixer until smooth. Add egg, egg yolk, butter extract, and maple syrup, mixing thoroughly with butter/sugar mixture.

3. Alternately add flour mixture and hot water to butter mixture, beating on low speed after each addition until combined. Spoon batter into prepared pan and spread evenly. Bake for 45 to 50 minutes, or until cake springs back when lightly touched. Remove from oven and let cool for 5 to 10 minutes. Using a butter knife, loosen cake sides and place on wire rack (sprayed with cooking spray) until cooled. Place cake on round platter or on cake stand.

4. Make icing by beating ½ cup powdered sugar and softened butter with electric mixer in medium bowl. Add pure maple syrup, and slowly beat in remaining 1 cup powdered sugar alternately with milk until smooth. Add vanilla and mix in. Spread icing on top and let drizzle down sides of cake.

5. Toast walnuts with brown sugar in dry skillet over medium heat, until sugar melts and walnuts become slightly brown, about 2 minutes. Stir walnuts often, being careful not to burn. Spread on waxed paper until cooled, and sprinkle over top of icing while still wet. Serves 8 to 10.

Cream Cheese Pound Cake with Strawberries

Cream Cheese Pound Cake with Strawberries

Note: *Pound cakes are popular in the southern cuisine and on any country table. Usually made with lots of butter and eggs, it is a rich dessert. This pound cake is a little different, using cream cheese, which makes it moist and quite delicious. Top with fresh strawberries, peaches, or raspberries for a lovely dessert.*

butter

flour

powdered sugar

1½ cups butter, softened slightly

1 (8-ounce) package cream cheese, softened

3 cups sugar

6 large eggs

3 cups all-purpose flour

¼ teaspoon salt

1 tablespoon vanilla extract

1 teaspoon almond extract

Vanilla Glaze

2 cups powdered sugar

4 to 5 tablespoons milk

2 teaspoons vanilla

½ cup fresh sweetened strawberries
   or fruit of choice

powdered sugar

mint leaves

1. Preheat oven to 300 degrees. Mix 2 tablespoons flour with 2 tablespoons powdered sugar and dust a buttered tube or Bundt pan; set aside.

2. In large mixing bowl, combine butter and cream cheese. Mix with electric mixer at medium speed until creamy. Gradually add sugar, beating until light and fluffy. Add eggs 1 at a time, beating just until blended after each addition.

3. Combine flour and salt; gradually add to butter mixture, beating at low speed just until blended. Stir in vanilla and almond extract and mix until blended.

4. Spoon batter into greased pan and spread evenly. Bake for 1 hour and 45 minutes, or until long wooden pick inserted in center comes out clean. Cake will crack on top, which is normal. Cool in pan on a wire rack 10 to 15 minutes; remove from pan, and let cool completely on wire rack. Place cake on pretty round cake platter or cake stand.

5. To make glaze, combine powdered sugar, milk, and vanilla in small bowl until thickened. Drizzle glaze around top and let it flow down sides. Top cake with sliced sweetened strawberries and dust lightly with powdered sugar. Garnish with mint leaves if desired. Serves 12.

Peach & Blueberry Shortcake

Peach & Blueberry Shortcake

Note: *A great treat in early and mid-summer when peaches and blueberries are fresh and plentiful. This shortcake is moist and has a wonderful light taste. This recipe works just as well with fresh cut strawberries.*

2 cups whipping cream

3 tablespoons sugar

2½ cups all-purpose flour

¼ cup sugar

4 teaspoons baking powder

½ cup butter, cut into pieces

2 large eggs, lightly beaten

½ cup sour cream

1 teaspoon vanilla extract

2 pounds fresh peaches

1 tablespoon lemon juice

½ cup sugar

¼ teaspoon ground nutmeg

1 teaspoon almond extract

1 tablespoon butter

1 cup fresh blueberries

whipped cream

peach wedges and blueberries

1. Preheat oven to 450 degrees. Pour whipping cream into a glass bowl and beat with electric mixer until foamy. Gradually beat in sugar at high speed until stiff peaks form. Cover and chill.

2. In large bowl, combine flour, sugar, and baking powder; cut in butter with a pastry blender or fork until crumbly. Stir together eggs, sour cream, and vanilla until blended; add to flour mixture, stirring just until dry ingredients are moistened.

3. Flour counter top and hands well to handle dough. Turn dough out onto floured counter top and turn a few times. Knead gently about 8 to 10 times. Roll dough into a 12-inch circle. Using a 3-inch biscuit cutter, cut into 15 rounds. Place rounds on a lightly greased baking sheet. Bake for 10 to 12 minutes or until golden. Remove from oven.

4. Cut peaches into wedges and sprinkle with lemon juice. Place peaches, sugar, nutmeg, and almond extract in medium saucepan. Cook over medium heat until bubbly, about 3 to 4 minutes. Remove from heat and add butter. Stir together until melted. Let cool slightly; add blueberries.

5. Remove shortcakes from baking pan; split rounds in half and lay bottom half in bowls. Divide fruit over bottom of rounds; top with some whipped cream. Put top of shortcake over fruit. Garnish with more whipped cream and a peach wedge or blueberries. Yields 15 shortcakes.

Strawberry Shortcake

1 quart strawberries, sliced

½ cup sugar

1. Combine sliced strawberries and ½ cup sugar; stir gently and chill 1 to 2 hours. Spread berries and juice over bottoms of shortcakes as above. Place a dollop of whipped cream over berries, then top with top of shortcake. Spoon more whipped cream over top and serve.

223

Rosalie's Blue Ribbon Carrot Cake

Rosalie's Blue Ribbon Carrot Cake

Note: *This cake is not only beautiful, but it is truly the best carrot cake I have ever served. You will love the moistness of this cake paired with the cream cheese frosting and topped with coconut and **Toasted Candied Pecans**. This is a dream!*

butter

flour

2 cups flour

2¼ cups sugar

2 teaspoons baking soda

1 teaspoon baking powder

½ teaspoon salt

2 teaspoons cinnamon

3 cups carrots, finely chopped or grated

4 eggs

1¼ cups mild olive oil

2 teaspoons vanilla

1 cup walnuts or pecans, finely chopped

1 cup raisins, optional

¾ cup soft coconut

Toasted Candied Pecans (see below)

Cream Cheese Frosting

2 (8-ounce) packages Philadelphia Cream
  Cheese, softened

½ cup butter

4 cups powdered sugar

1 teaspoons vanilla

Toasted Candied Pecans

½ cup whole pecans

1 tablespoon sugar

1. Preheat oven to 350 degrees. Butter and flour three 9-inch cake pans. In large bowl, combine flour, sugar, baking soda, baking powder, salt and cinnamon. Add the carrots and mix. Add the eggs, oil, vanilla, walnuts, and raisins. Blend well and pour the batter into the cake pans.

2. Bake for 30 minutes, or until cake bounces back when touched. Cool on wire racks for 10 minutes. Remove from pans and continue to cool on racks (sprayed with cooking spray) until completely cooled.

3. Prepare **Cream Cheese Frosting** by combining cream cheese, butter, powdered sugar, and vanilla; stir together well. Place first cake layer top-side down on cake stand and frost. Continue with second layer. Place third layer top-side up and continue to frost sides and top of cake.

4. Place coconut around top edge of cake and inward about 2 inches. Place pecans in dry skillet with sugar added. Toast about 2 to 3 minutes, stirring often. Place the **Toasted Candied Pecans** in a row around the inner circle of the top layer. Place a large maraschino cherry in the center.

5. Refrigerate until ready to serve. Serves 12 to 16.

225

Pumpkin Walnut Swirl Cheesecake

Note: *This cheesecake is wonderful to serve around Thanksgiving time, but is delicious for any occasion. The ginger snaps give it an extra bounce of flavor and compliments the pumpkin. A beautiful presentation garnished with candied walnuts and caramel topping, you will be proud to serve this lovely dessert.*

2 cups Ginger Snaps, finely crushed

¼ cup brown sugar

½ cup walnuts, finely chopped

½ cup butter, melted

4 (8-ounce) packages cream cheese

1 cup sugar

2 teaspoons vanilla

4 eggs

1 cup canned pumpkin

⅓ cup brown sugar

⅓ cup granulated sugar

1½ teaspoons ground cinnamon

¼ teaspoon ground nutmeg

¼ teaspoon ground cloves

Sour Cream Topping

1 pint sour cream

¼ cup sugar

1 teaspoon lemon juice

Toasted Candied Walnuts

1 cup walnuts, coarsely chopped

2 tablespoons sugar

⅓ cup Hershey's Caramel Topping

1. Preheat oven to 325 degrees. Mix Ginger Snap crumbs, brown sugar, walnuts, and butter. With the bottom of a cup or juice glass, pat the crumb mixture up the sides of a 9-inch springform pan, leaving a ½ -inch crust on the bottom. Place in freezer for 8 to 10 minutes to chill.

2. Beat cream cheese, sugar, and vanilla with electric mixer or food processor until well blended. Add eggs, one at a time, mixing on low speed after each addition just until blended.

3. Remove 1½ cups batter; place in small bowl. In medium bowl, combine pumpkin, brown sugar, granulated sugar, cinnamon, nutmeg, and cloves, pour into remaining batter. Spoon half of the pumpkin batter into crust; top with spoonfuls of half of the reserved plain batter. Repeat layers. Cut through batters with knife several times for marble effect.

4. Bake 1 hour and 10 minutes or until center is set. Let cheesecake cool completely; run knife around edge and remove outer pan. Place a cookie sheet or round platter over top of cheesecake. Flip cheesecake over and remove bottom pan. Flip cake back over onto a large round decorative platter or cake stand so that the cookie crust is on the bottom.

5. Prepare topping by combining sour cream, sugar and lemon juice. Spread over top of cheesecake. Make toasted candied walnuts by placing walnuts and sugar in dry skillet over low heat, stirring constantly. Toast the walnuts about 2 minutes until aromatic and slightly browned. Remove and sprinkle over sour cream topping. Drizzle the caramel topping over the walnuts. Keep cheesecake refrigerated until ready to serve. Makes 16 servings.

Pumpkin Walnut Swirl Cheesecake

Dark Chocolate Raspberry Cheesecake

Note: *This cheesecake is a huge towering beauty that looks like it belongs in the window of a very elite bakery. With plenty of the dark chocolate frosting on the top and raspberry preserves for garnish, it is truly a salivating experience. For a grand chocolate cheesecake, this is it!*

2 cups Oreo cookies
6 tablespoons butter

6 (8- ounce) packages cream cheese
2 cups sugar
6 eggs

3 cups Special Dark Chocolate Chips
3 tablespoons half-and-half or evaporated milk
2 teaspoons vanilla

Dark Chocolate Topping

½ cup Special Dark Chocolate Chips
⅓ cup evaporated milk

1 (8-ounce) jar raspberry preserves
powdered sugar
pressurized whipped cream
½ cup fresh red raspberries, optional

1. Preheat oven to 350-degrees. Using a blender or food processor, chop cookies very fine. Place cookie crumbs in medium bowl. Melt butter and stir into crumbs until the mixture comes together. With the bottom of a cup or juice glass, pat the crumb mixture up the sides of a 10-inch springform pan, leaving a ½-inch crust on the bottom. Place in freezer for 8 to 10 minutes to chill.

2. In food processor or large mixing bowl, combine cream cheese and sugar. Mix together on medium setting until creamy and smooth. Add eggs one at a time, beating well after each addition. Melt chocolate and milk in small heavy pot, slowly stirring until smooth. Pour chocolate and vanilla into cheese mixture, and blend thoroughly. Pour into prepared crust, and bake for about 1 hour and 20 minutes or until set. Cheesecake may crack on top.

3. Let cheesecake cool; remove outer pan. Place a cookie sheet or large round platter over top of cheesecake. Flip cheesecake over and remove bottom pan. Flip cake back over onto a large round decorative platter so that the cookie crust is on the bottom.

4. For **Dark Chocolate Topping,** melt chocolate chips gently over very low heat and stir in the milk to a thin consistency. Spread over top and sides of cake and let set, or put in refrigerator until chocolate hardens. Spoon raspberry preserves into small bowl and place in micro-wave for few seconds to slightly thin preserves. Spoon over top of chocolate, starting in the middle of the cake and spreading within a 2-inch border of the edge of the cake. Lightly dust with powdered sugar over top. Flute the edge of cake with whipping cream, and garnish with fresh raspberries if desired. Keep refrigerated until time to serve cake. Serves 16.

Sheraton's Famous Cheesecake

Note: *I received this recipe from a dear friend years ago and always reserved it for my special catering occasions. Rumor has it that this cheesecake was once on the menu at the exclusive Sheraton Hotel in St. Louis, Missouri. It is the favorite Christmas dessert of all three of my children and their spouses. Served with **Pineapple Sauce,** (see below) this dessert is truly a "mouthful of bliss."*

2 cups graham cracker crumbs

¼ cup sugar

½ cup melted butter

4 (8-ounce) packages of cream cheese

4 eggs

1 cup plus 2 tablespoons sugar

1 teaspoon vanilla

Sour Cream Topping

1 (8-ounce) carton sour cream

¼ cup sugar

1 teaspoon lemon juice

1. Preheat oven to 325 degrees. Combine graham cracker crumbs, sugar, and butter in a small bowl; mix together. With the bottom of a cup or juice glass, pat the crumb mixture up the sides of a 10-inch springform or a 10-inch deep pie pan, leaving a ½-inch crust on the bottom. Set aside.

2. In large mixing bowl, beat cream cheese with electric mixer until smooth. Add eggs, one at a time, beating after each addition. Add sugar and vanilla, and continue beating until blended to a satin-like mixture. Pour filling over crust. Bake 1 hour and 10 minutes or until set in the middle. Cheese cake will form cracks on top. Remove from oven and let cool completely.

3. If using a springform pan run knife around edge and remove outer pan. Place a cookie sheet or round platter over top of cheesecake. Flip cheesecake over and remove bottom pan. Flip cake back over onto a large round decorative platter or cake stand so that the crust is on the bottom.

4. Make **Sour Cream Topping** by combining sour cream, sugar and lemon juice. Spread evenly over top of cheesecake. Chill at least 4 hours before serving. Serve plain or with **Pineapple Sauce.**

Pineapple Sauce

1 (20-ounce) can crushed pineapple, undrained

2 tablespoons cornstarch

⅓ cup sugar

½ teaspoon vanilla

2 tablespoons butter

1. Mix pineapple, cornstarch, sugar and vanilla in a bowl until cornstarch and sugar have dissolved. Pour into saucepan and over medium heat, bring mixture to a gentle boil; add butter. Lower heat while stirring constantly until mixture thickens. Remove from heat and bring to room temperature. Serve over **Sheraton's Famous Cheesecake.**

229

Turnpike Cheesecake

Note: *I created this cheesecake in honor of the birth of my tenth grandchild, Sebastian Durniat Schultz, who was born in the back seat of the family car on a Florida Turnpike. With the flavor of the traditional Key lime pie, this luscious dessert boasts a twist of orange and coconut graham cracker crust to resemble a tropical cheesecake that is quite delicious.*

2 cups cinnamon graham crackers
1 cup shredded coconut
⅓ cup brown sugar
½ cup butter, melted

2 (8-ounce) packages cream cheese
1 can sweetened condensed milk
½ cup fresh lime juice
1 teaspoon grated lime peel
⅓ cup fresh orange juice
½ teaspoon grated orange peel

Meringue

6 egg whites at room temperature
1 teaspoon cream of tartar
⅓ cup sugar

coconut, optional

1. Preheat oven to 325 degrees. In food processor, pulse the graham crackers, coconut, and brown sugar until crackers are reduced to crumbs; pour in the butter and pulse again until crumbs are coated with butter.

2. Place the graham cracker mixture in a 9-inch springform pan. With the bottom of a cup or juice glass, pat the graham cracker mixture up the sides of the pan, leaving a ½-inch crust on the bottom. Place in freezer for 8 to 10 minutes to chill.

3. In food processor or electric mixer bowl, place the cream cheese, condensed milk, lime juice, lime peel, orange juice, and orange peel. Pulse on medium high until creamy and smooth. Pour cheese mixture into the graham cracker crust; set aside.

4. In a large mixing bowl, place the egg whites, and with an electric mixer, beat whites until soft peaks form, about 4 minutes. Add the cream of tartar and the sugar a little at a time; continue to beat on high until stiff peaks form. Pour meringue over top of cheesecake; sprinkle with coconut if desired.

5. Place cheesecake in oven and bake for 45 to 50 minutes; meringue will be golden brown. Cool cake on rack for 30 minutes. Remove outer pan and let cake cool completely. Remove bottom pan from cake using a large spatula and place on platter or cake stand. Keep cake refrigerated until ready to serve. Serves 12.

Turnpike Cheesecake

Turtle Dove Pecan Cheesecake

Note: *This cheesecake is one of a kind, and one you will hold in your memory forever. Created for a Valentine's Day special, it is a rich combination of caramel, pecans, and chocolate combined into a cheesecake. It is so yummy; you'll want to make it for more than just one occasion.*

4 cups chocolate graham cracker crumbs
⅓ cup brown sugar
¾ cup butter, melted

4 (8-ounce) packages cream cheese
1¼ cups sugar
3 tablespoons lime juice
1 tablespoon vanilla extract
4 eggs

1½ cups semi-sweet chocolate morsels
3 tablespoons evaporated milk

Chocolate Topping

1 (6-ounce) package semi-sweet
   chocolate morsels
⅓ to ½ cup sweetened condensed milk

½ cup Hershey's Caramel Topping

Toasted Candied Pecans

1 cup whole pecans
1 tablespoon sugar

whipped cream

1. Preheat oven to 350 degrees. Place graham crackers, brown sugar, and butter in a food processor or blender until well blended. With the bottom of a cup or juice glass, pat the crumb mixture up the sides of a buttered 10-inch springform pan. Chill in the freezer 8 to 10 minutes while making the filling.

2. In a food processor or mixer, beat the cream cheese, sugar, lime juice, and vanilla until smooth. Add the eggs one at a time, mixing after each addition. Remove 2 cups cream cheese batter and place in medium bowl; set aside.

3. Mix chocolate morsels and evaporated milk in small heavy pot. Turn heat to low and mix chocolate with milk stirring constantly until melted and smooth. Add the chocolate mixture to the 2 cups cream cheese batter and stir together until blended.

4. Remove crust from freezer. Alternately spoon batters into crust beginning and ending with plain batter. Swirl gently to make a marble effect. Bake for 1 hour, or until cake is set. Cool in pan on wire rack for 10 minutes; run knife around edge and carefully remove outer pan. Let cheesecake cool completely before garnishing top.

5. When cake is set and cooled, place a cookie sheet or round platter over top of cheesecake. Flip cheesecake over and remove bottom pan. Flip cake back over onto large round platter.

6. Prepare **Chocolate Topping** by placing chocolate morsels and condensed milk in small heavy pot. Over low heat, mix chocolate with milk, stirring constantly until melted and smooth. Let cool; spread chocolate over top of cheesecake to the edge. Place caramel topping in microwave for a few seconds if too stiff. Drizzle caramel topping in lines back and forth over chocolate, letting some drip off the sides of cake.

7. Place pecans in dry skillet and add sugar. Over medium heat, stir often until pecans become aromatic and toasted, about 2 minutes. Place **Toasted Candied Pecans** in center circle of cheesecake. Keep cheesecake refrigerated until ready to serve, at least 3 to 4 hours. Flute edge of cheesecake with whipped cream and serve. Serves 16.

Almond Crescents

Note: *If you like cinnamon and almonds, these cookies will delight you as well as your guests. This great melt-in-your-mouth cookie, is wonderful at Christmas or any occasion.*

½ cup butter, softened
½ Crisco shortening
⅓ cup granulated sugar
⅔ cup ground blanched almonds

1⅔ cup all-purpose flour
¼ teaspoon salt

1 cup granulated sugar
2 tablespoons ground cinnamon

1. Preheat oven to 325 degrees. In mixing bowl, cream butter, shortening and sugar with electric mixer. Add the ground almonds and mix in well.

2. With clean hands, mix in the flour and salt. Pinch off pieces of dough and roll into small crescent shapes; place on ungreased baking sheets. Bake until set, but not brown, about 14 to 16 minutes.

3. Combine the sugar and cinnamon and place in a shallow bowl. While crescents are still warm, gently remove and roll carefully in the cinnamon sugar. Place on pretty platter and serve, or keep in covered container until ready to serve. Yields about 3 dozen cookies.

Old World Raspberry Bars

Note: *These raspberry bars are one of the best bar cookies I have ever tasted. They are positively delicious, and very easy to make up. You can store them in an air-tight container very nicely—if you can get them that far. Just the smell of these freshly baked delights will have your family gathered around the oven immediately.*

2¼ cups all-purpose flour

1 cup granulated sugar

1 cup pecans, finely chopped

1 cup sweet butter, softened

1 egg

butter

1 (10-ounce) jar raspberry preserves

1. Preheat oven to 350 degrees. In a 3-quart mixing bowl, combine flour, sugar, pecans, butter and egg. Mix together until mixture is crumbly. Set aside 1½ cups of crumb mixture.

2. Butter a 13 by 9-inch pan and press remaining crumb mixture into pan. Spread the preserves to within ½-inch of edges. Crumble the reserved crumb mixture over preserves. Bake bars in center of oven for 35 to 40 minutes or until lightly browned. Yields about 2 dozen bars.

"Something Special" Sugar Cookies

Note: *This could be the best Christmas sugar cookie ever! Whether using buttercream frosting with almond flavor, or sugar sprinkles, you won't be able to eat just one. Yummy!*

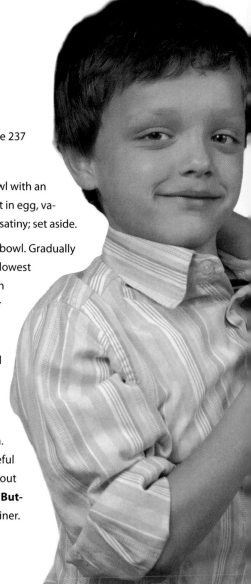

1 cup butter, softened
1½ cups granulated sugar
1 egg
1½ teaspoons vanilla extract
1 teaspoon almond extract

2¾ cups all-purpose flour
½ teaspoon baking powder
1 teaspoon salt

1 **Buttercream Frosting** recipe found on page 237

1. Preheat oven to 350 degrees. In a large bowl with an electric mixer, cream butter and sugar. Beat in egg, vanilla and almond extract until smooth and satiny; set aside.

2. Mix flour, baking powder, and salt in large bowl. Gradually mix in the butter/sugar mixture, using the lowest speed. With floured hands bring the dough together. Cut dough a portion at a time for easier handling, and roll out. Dip cookie cutters in flour or powdered sugar before cutting out designs. This dough works well in a cookie press or rolled out for cutouts.

3. With a flat turner, transfer cookie cutouts to an ungreased baking sheet; sprinkle with sugar sprinkles, or leave cookies plain. Bake cookies for 6 to 8 minutes, being careful not to burn. Cookies will continue to cook out of oven. Cool. Decorate plain cookies with **Buttercream Frosting.** Store in airtight container. Yields 2 to 3 dozen cookies.

Buttercream Frosting

Note: *This frosting is great on cookies or cakes. Is has a delightful butter-almond flavor that can enhance many desserts. See below for variations.*

1½ cups butter, softened
4 cups sifted powdered sugar
2 tablespoons half-and-half
1 teaspoon almond extract

1. Cream butter at medium speed with an electric mixer; gradually add sugar, beating until light and fluffy. Add half-and-half and beat until spreading consistency. Add more liquid if needed. Stir in almond extract. Spread frosting as desired. Yields 3 cups.

Buttercream Orange Frosting

1. Substitute 2 to 3 tablespoons orange juice for milk, and use vanilla extract for almond. To add a taste of spice, add 1 teaspoon of ground cinnamon and ¼ teaspoon of ground cloves.

Buttercream Chocolate Frosting

1. Add ¼ cup cocoa when adding sugar to the **Buttercream Frosting.**

Grant and Max Harpole

237

Chocolate Covered Cherry Cookies

Rosalie Serving Country

Chocolate Covered Cherry Cookies

Note: *I make these cookies every Christmas because they are one of my daughter's favorites. These cookies taste like candied chocolate covered cherries. They are rich with chocolate topping and the cookie dough is soft and delicious. A great cookie for the holidays or any occasion.*

2¼ cups all-purpose flour
½ cup unsweetened cocoa
¼ teaspoon salt
¼ teaspoon baking powder
¼ teaspoon baking soda

1 cup butter
1 cup sugar
1 egg
1½ teaspoon vanilla
1 (10-ounce) jar maraschino cherries

1 (6-ounce) package semisweet
   chocolate morsels
½ cup condensed milk
4 to 5 teaspoons reserved cherry juice
powered sugar, optional

1. Preheat oven to 350 degrees. In large bowl, stir together flour, cocoa, salt, baking powder, and baking soda.

2. Cream together butter and sugar until fluffy. Add egg and vanilla; beat well. Gradually add flour mixture. Shape dough into small balls and place on cookie sheet. Press down center of each ball with thumb. Drain cherries and put ½ cherry in center of each cookie. Bake cookies on ungreased cookie sheet 8 to 10 minutes.

3. In small saucepan, combine chocolate morsels and milk. Heat over low heat until chocolate melts, and milk and chocolate are smooth. Add the cherry juice and stir together well. Remove cookies from oven. Spoon chocolate topping over top of each cookie while still warm, and place on cookie sheet. Let cool and remove to cookie platter. Dust lightly with powered sugar, if desired. Cookies can be frozen in zip-lock air-tight bags. Yields 3 to 4 dozen.

Extraordinary Chocolate Chip Cookies

Note: *These chocolate chip cookies could be the best I have ever found. Since this batch makes a large amount, you will want to keep them in an air-tight container to keep fresh. If you are like my family, you'll have to discard that idea.*

1½ cups butter
1¼ cups granulated sugar
1¼ cups packed brown sugar
1 tablespoon vanilla
2 eggs

4 cups all-purpose flour
2 teaspoons baking soda
½ teaspoon salt

1 (24-ounce) bag semisweet chocolate chips

1. Preheat oven to 350 degrees. In large mixing bowl, beat butter and sugars until light and fluffy. Add vanilla and eggs and continue to beat, until thoroughly mixed.

2. Combine flour, backing soda, and salt. Stir into butter and sugar mixture. Add chocolate chips and with clean hands, mix together; dough may be stiff.

3. On ungreased cookie sheet, drop dough by tablespoon, or use a small ice cream scoop, 2-inches apart; flatten slightly.

4. Bake 10 to 12 minutes or until lightly browned. Centers will be soft, but cookies continue to cook even after removal from oven. Cool on cookie sheet, and then remove to large platter. Makes about 6 dozen cookies.

Sugared Pecan Balls

Note: *These melt-in-your mouth dreams are just the right cookie for your tea or club parties. You can make them up in no time and they look beautiful on your platter. They are the ever-favorite cookie, called by many names, and can be found in most family recipe books.*

1 cup butter, room temperature

5 tablespoons granulated sugar

½ teaspoon salt

2 cups ground pecans

2 cups all-purpose flour

3 teaspoons vanilla

2 cups powdered sugar

1. Preheat oven to 325 degrees. Cream butter, sugar, and salt until smooth. Add the pecans, flour and vanilla, using your hands to mix thoroughly. Form dough into small balls and place on ungreased cookie sheet. Bake for 15 to 20 minutes. Watch cookies closely; they are done when brown on bottom.

2. Roll the cookies while still warm in powdered sugar, being careful not to break. Place on cookie platter and sift additional powdered sugar over cookies. For a colorful Christmas cookie, add a few drops red or green food coloring to dough. Makes about 6 dozen cookies, depending on the size of the balls.

241

Elijah Schultz

Nicholas Harpole

Candied Popcorn

Note: *A great treat for the holidays or any time. This recipe makes a big pan for the whole family, or can be stored in gallon zip-lock bags for later use or for gifts. Be sure to pop the popcorn in mild olive oil for a great taste.*

butter

6 quarts freshly popped popcorn (unsalted)

1 cup raw peanuts

2 cups whole pecans

1¼ cups butter

2 cups firmly packed brown sugar

½ cup dark corn syrup

½ teaspoon baking soda

½ teaspoon salt

½ teaspoon vanilla extract

1. Preheat oven to 250 degrees. Place popcorn, peanuts, and pecans in a lightly buttered large roasting pan; set mixture aside.

2. Melt butter in a 3-quart heavy saucepan; stir in sugar and corn syrup. Bring mixture to a boil, and continue to boil for 5 minutes, stirring often. Remove from heat; stir in soda, salt, and vanilla.

3. Pour sugar mixture over popcorn; stir well to coat. Bake for 1 hour, stirring every 15 minutes. Cool; store in an airtight container. Yields 6 quarts.

(Time: 10 Minutes)

Olive Oil Popcorn

3 tablespoons olive oil

½ cup Orville Redenbacher's popping corn

salt

1. Pour the olive oil and popcorn into a heavy pot. Cover and over medium heat pop the corn, occasionally shaking the pan from side to side. When kernels stop popping, carefully remove lid. Transfer to a large bowl. Add desired amount of salt and serve. Makes 10 cups.

244

Honeycomb Peanut Brittle

Note: *This is the famous peanut brittle that has been so popular for many years, not only in the South, but everywhere. Many churches use it for fund raisers and every winter people buy it, not only for the purpose of contributing to a great cause, but just because it is so delicious. Everyone can eat it because it has a foamy center much like a honeycomb. The only problem? No one can eat just one bag. . .it is so addictive!*

3 heaping teaspoons baking soda

1 teaspoon salt

1 (18 by 24-inch) piece of heavy aluminum foil,
   buttered

large pot of boiling water

3 cups C & H sugar

1 cup white corn syrup

½ cup water

2 cups raw Spanish peanuts

2 tablespoons butter or Imperial margarine

1. Combine the baking soda and salt in a small bowl; set aside. Cover a piece of cardboard with the foil to avoid burning table top, or work on a stainless steel table or large cookie sheet.

2. In a 3-quart heavy pot, combine sugar, corn syrup and water. Over medium high heat, stir the mixture with a long wooden spoon until the sugar is dissolved. Bring to boil and using a candy thermometer, bring mixture to 230 degrees, cooking for about 5 minutes. The syrup will turn a clear crystal texture and when lifting spoon coated with syrup, threads of syrup will hang from the spoon.

3. Add the peanuts and continue cooking until mixture reaches 310 degrees, or hard-crack stage. Stir often with the long wooden spoon. From the time the peanuts are added, cook another 5 minutes until the syrup mixture turns a golden caramel color. Add the 2 tablespoons of butter and continue stirring the pot until the butter melts, about 30 seconds.

4. Remove from heat and add the baking soda and salt mixture all at once. Stir vigorously to diffuse the baking soda. Let the brittle "foam up" in the pot, being careful not to let it spill over the top. Pour the brittle onto the buttered foil in a back and forth motion to form a large rectangle of brittle. DO NOT TOUCH THE HOT BRITTLE. Immediately place the pot and spoon in a large pot of boiling water, very carefully, to clean the pot.

5. Let the brittle completely harden and cool, about 45 minutes. The brittle will come off the foil easily when completely cooled. Break the brittle in chunks and place about 10 ounces in a 1-quart plastic bag. Seal the bag for freshness. Recipe makes about 3½ (10-ounces) bags.

Note: For the best outcome making peanut brittle, make it on a cold, dry day. This candy does not set up in spring and summer months, and does not do well in rainy weather. Also be very careful making peanut brittle; one splash on skin will result in a serious burn. Always use a long handle spoon, preferably wooden, and large hot pads or gloves to protect hands.

245

Taylor & Ross Harpole

Creamy Marshmallow Fudge

Note: *There are so many recipes for fudge, but if you are looking for a no-fail quick fudge that is creamy and delicious, this is it. Add toasted sweetened walnuts to make it even better.*

1 ½ cups sugar

⅔ cup undiluted evaporated milk,
  (1 small can)

¼ cup butter

1 jar marshmallow cream, about 7 ounces,
  or 16 large marshmallows

¼ teaspoon salt

Toasted Walnuts

1 cup walnuts, coarsely chopped

3 teaspoons brown sugar

1 (12-ounce) package semi-sweet
  chocolate chips

1 teaspoon vanilla

1. In 3-quart heavy saucepan, combine sugar, evaporated milk, butter, marshmallow cream or marshmallows, and salt. Cook over medium heat, stirring constantly, until mixture has boiled for exactly 5 minutes.

2. Toast, walnuts and sugar in dry hot skillet, 1 to 2 minutes, until sugar melts and walnuts become slightly browned and aromatic.

3. Remove from heat and add chocolate chips and vanilla; stir until chocolate is melted. Stir in the toasted walnuts. Spoon mixture into a buttered 8-inch square pan. Let stand until firm, then cut into squares. Makes about 1½ dozen, 2-inch squares.

Heavenly Hash

Note: *This candy is so good you will want to make it for all your special occasions. Great wrapped up for gifts or just to have around when the special guests come calling. This should be called "disappearing" Heavenly Hash.*

1 (12-ounce) package semi-sweet chocolate chips
1 (15-ounce) can sweetened condensed milk

1 (10.5-ounce) package or 6 cups miniature marshmallows
1 cup pecans, coarsely chopped

1. In large saucepan melt chocolate chips over very low heat; stir until smooth. Turn off burner and slowly add condensed milk. Stir until milk and chocolate are blended.

2. Add the marshmallows and pecans, mixing until marshmallows and pecans are well coated. Drop by tablespoons onto a waxed paper-lined cookie sheet. Refrigerate until firm. Makes 3 dozen pieces of candy.

David & Sebastian Schultz

INDEX:

Index:

Index:

Rosalie Serving Country

255

GENERAL INDEX:

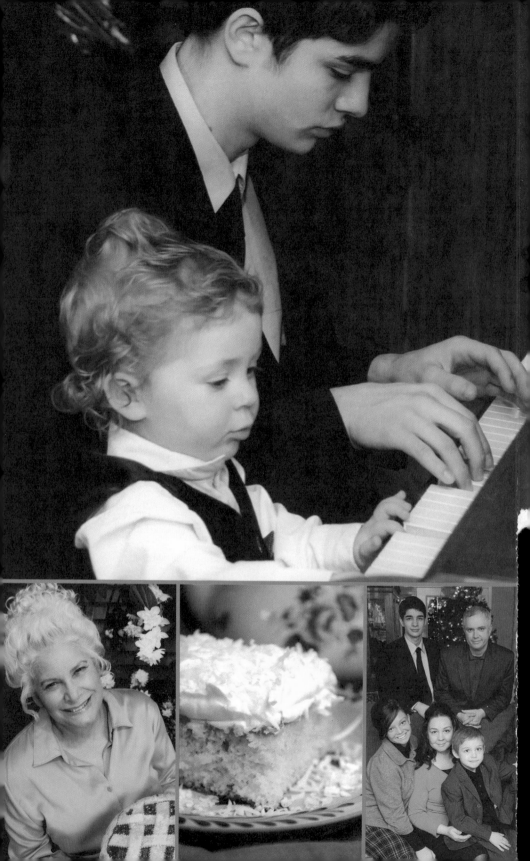